Advance Praise for *The Right* CEO

"Selecting a CEO is the most important of all board responsibilities. This book should be required reading for all stakeholders before launching that process."
—**James L. Vincent**, chairman of the board, Biogen

"Fred Wackerle's book is both comprehensive and insightful. It should be a ready reference for any board member, incumbent CEO, human resource executive or CEO search consultant who wants clear, sound, practical advice on how to make those tough CEO selection decisions."
—**Lewis Campbell**, chairman, Textron, Inc.

"Fred Wackerle clearly succeeds in demythologizing the process for selecting The Right CEO. His book contains wisdom for the board, the search consultant, the HR officer, the incumbent CEO, and the candidate, too. The inter-relationships among all these participants are the key to the right decision and a successful transition."
—**Fred G. Steingraber,** chairman emeritus, A.T. Kearney

"Fred Wackerle, the quintessential professional and consultant, has written a book that will become the conscience for all of us involved in CEO selection. Fred captures the essentials of what really happens. . . . He's been there. He reveals the myths of the CEO succession process and why today it is broken. The book is must reading for anyone who cares about the future of corporate leadership."
—**Roger M. Kenny,** managing partner, Boardroom Consultants

The Right CEO

Frederick W. Wackerle

Foreword by William W. George

The Right CEO

Straight Talk About Making Tough CEO Selection Decisions

JOSSEY-BASS
A Wiley Company
www.josseybass.com

Published by

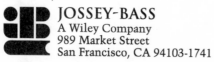 **JOSSEY-BASS**
A Wiley Company
989 Market Street
San Francisco, CA 94103-1741

www.josseybass.com

Jossey-Bass books and products are available through most bookstores. To contact Jossey-Bass directly, call (888) 378-2537, fax to (800) 605-2665, or visit our website at www.josseybass.com.

Substantial discounts on bulk quantities of Jossey-Bass books are available to corporations, professional associations, and other organizations. For details and discount information, contact the special sales department at Jossey-Bass.

We at Jossey-Bass strive to use the most environmentally sensitive paper stocks available to us. Our publications are printed on acid-free recycled stock whenever possible, and our paper always meets or exceeds minimum GPO and EPA requirements.

Library of Congress Cataloging-in-Publication Data

Wackerle, Frederick W., 1939-
    The right CEO : straight talk about making tough CEO selection decisions / Frederick W. Wackerle ; foreword by William W. George.— 1st ed.
        p. cm. — (The Jossey-Bass business & management series)
Includes index.
    ISBN 0-7879-5585-X (alk. paper)
    1. Chief executive officers—Selection and appointment.   I. Title.   II. Series.
HF5549.5.R44 W33 2001
658.4'07112—dc21   2001003793

FIRST EDITION
HB Printing   10 9 8 7 6 5 4 3 2 1

The Jossey-Bass

Business & Management Series

For Barbara, Jennifer, and Ruth

Contents

Foreword

Virtually every week the newspapers bring us word of yet another relatively new CEO who fails at a major corporation. Most of these people have been carefully selected through a thorough screening and evaluation process. They have been highly successful at each stage of their careers up to now. Yet the process ends in failure. What's going on here?

In this extremely valuable primer on CEO selection, Fred Wackerle describes this process in vivid detail. He draws upon his immense experience, using numerous case histories to illustrate how the process works and what can go wrong. This exposition could not be more timely: We need to get the process right if our great corporations are going to prosper over the long term.

I am a fortunate beneficiary of the process working well, thanks in large measure to the skill of the author. I had never met Fred before the summer of 1988. That July I received a telephone call from him. He described a very interesting opportunity for me with Medtronic in which I would join the company as president and chief operating officer and be in line to succeed Win Wallin as chief executive officer when he planned to retire in two years.

At the time I was running the Space and Aviation Systems at Honeywell. I had uncovered a huge set of overruns in the company's military avionics business, largely at the recently acquired Sperry Military Avionic operation in Albuquerque, New Mexico. I envisioned myself as a strong candidate to run Honeywell, where I had been an executive for the past ten years. So I told Fred there was no way I could make the move to Medtronic. Fred encouraged me "to keep the door open" in case my situation changed.

It did. By mid-fall the problems were not only fully identified but corrective actions were well under way. I had decided that perhaps the Medtronic culture, with its commitment to the mission of "restoring people to full life and health," would be a better fit for me than Honeywell. So this time I initiated the call to Fred to see whether the position was still open. Fred explained that Medtronic was pretty far down the line with another candidate but that he would like to get me involved.

From then on Fred took charge. He quickly organized the process, was extremely sensitive to confidentiality and my busy travel schedule, and worked effectively as a middleman between the company and myself. Fred did an outstanding job of coordinating among Win Wallin, Lowell Jacobsen (Medtronic's senior vice president of human resources), the Medtronic board, and me. He even was skillful enough to convince Earl Bakken, Medtronic's founder who was living in Hawaii, to fly from Kona to Phoenix, Arizona, for a confidential interview with me.

At the point it was clear that Medtronic wanted me for the position but I had not finally made up my mind to leave Honeywell, Fred took on a new role. He offered to be *my counselor*. Fred proposed to act as my intermediary with the company to ensure that I was satisfied with all the details of the position and the offer. I eventually accepted the job in March and started in early April.

Thus began a long and highly successful relationship among Fred, Medtronic, and me. We were so pleased with the sensitive way he had handled the entire process that we used Fred to help us recruit Art Collins as my successor as COO and now CEO and Bob Ryan, Medtronic's current CFO, along with several other key executives.

I share this personal story to illustrate how well the process can work when the search consultant is really skilled and sensitive to the needs of all of the parties highlighted in this book: the incumbent CEO, the board, the CHRO, and the CEO candidates.

Unfortunately, it often doesn't work this way, and the process gets off track: There are power and political struggles between the board and the incumbent CEO about the type of candidate required; and the wrong candidate is selected, or no candidate at all. In recent years many CEOs have been recruited to top jobs, only to find themselves out of a job in less than two years.

This book is filled with dozens of real-life examples, some of them disguised, some not, and lots of "straight talk" from the author in describing how well-intentioned people can get off track and the process can go awry. Throughout this book, Fred is nothing if not candid. It is in this candor that the reader comes to appreciate the subtleties of the process and the intricacy of managing all the personalities involved to achieve a successful conclusion: choosing the right CEO.

It is my hope that this book will be a turning point and catalyze a vitally needed reassessment of the CEO selection process in corporate America. If it does, we will all be grateful to Fred Wackerle for his candor and the clarity of his insights, as well as his recommended improvements.

July 2001　　　　　　　　　　　　　　　William W. George
Minneapolis, Minnesota　　　　　　　　Chairman, Medtronic, Inc.

Introduction

Organizations seem to have lost the knack for selecting the right CEO successors. The business press regularly reports on CEOs who have failed, having either resigned in disgrace or been booted out by their boards. The executive search business is booming because companies have failed to develop their internal talent; as a result, their succession plans are nonexistent or have not yielded viable candidates. The cost of these failures is enormous.

Hewlett-Packard committed close to $90 million (salary, benefits, bonus, and stock options) of stockholders' money to recruit Carly Fiorina as their new CEO because they had been unable to develop internal successors. Coca-Cola and Procter & Gamble lost valuable momentum during an economic boom because they made poor decisions in selecting a CEO from inside. Organizations can waste years not only searching for the right candidate but also re-searching after the selected CEO proves unsuited to the requirements of the job. In addition to lost time, money, and momentum, companies lose valuable talent when the CEO selection process goes awry. Alienated executives who thought they should have been given consideration leave in disgust. A chief operating officer (COO) who feels the CEO misled him into believing that the top job would soon be his begins looking at a company that will make him their CEO. Other executive talent, fed up with a lack of sound leadership and a board that can't get CEO selection right, looks for work at better-led organizations.

It doesn't have to be this way. In the following chapters, I'll identify the flaws in the current CEO selection process and suggest ways they can be addressed. But this book is not just about *how to* but *how come*. To make the right selection, you need to understand why organizations fail to find the right CEOs, given their requirements. To impart this understanding, I'll explore the behaviors of board members, incumbent CEOs, human resources executives, CEO search consultants, and candidates. These five players are part of a delicate dynamic that can be upset by dysfunctional behaviors exhibited by any one of them. Much of my focus will be on the actions of boards and incumbent CEOs, examining how boards fail to live up to their stewardship responsibilities and incumbent CEOs commit the sin of hubris. As we'll see, these and other actions make selecting the right CEO extremely difficult.

At the same time, some organizations are quite astute about CEO succession and selection. They have figured out how to achieve the proper balance among all five process participants and end up making extraordinary effective CEO selections. I'll share examples of companies that have done it right and offer various suggestions about how any organization can follow these examples.

How My Experiences Shaped This Book

I've spent over thirty-five years in the executive search consulting profession. I began my career at the management consulting firm of A. T. Kearney and eventually co-founded my own executive search consulting firm with Clarence McFeely. During my career, I conducted many CEO and other top executive searches for companies such as MassMutual, General Electric, Citicorp, Textron, Medtronic, Fruit of the Loom, Owens Corning, Playboy Enterprises, IMC Global, Biogen, GATX, FMC, General Instruments, Outboard Marine, and Whirlpool. Today, I am retired from "searching" but continue to advise CEOs and boards on selection and succession issues.

During my time in the search profession, things have changed. I'd like to give you a brief history of those changes because they help explain why it's so difficult for companies to select the right

CEOs today. In the 1950s and 1960s, executive search professionals were part of consulting firms such as A. T. Kearney, Booz Allen & Hamilton, and George Fry. Major accounting firms, too, got into the executive search act. This was a natural business extension for both types of firms, since their clients reflexively asked for their advice about finding a new CFO (accounting firms) or CEO (consulting firms). Independent executive search consultancies soon opened their offices, including Haley Associates, Heidrick & Struggles, Spencer Stuart, and Boyden Associates.

Still, executive search consulting was an "underground" industry for many years. It was not until the 1980s that hiring a search consulting firm became a publicly acceptable practice. Up until the 1960s or even the 1970s, many companies felt it was an admission of failure to hire this type of consultant, especially if the search was for the company's top position. Even though organizations did use executive search consultants during this time, they rarely talked about it to the media and often limited the search consultants' assignments to non-CEO positions.

If there was a singular event that cemented the search consultant's role in the CEO selection process, it was the publicity surrounding Lawton Johnson of Boyden Associates in recruiting Harold Gineen to ITT. Lawton's recruitment of Gineen as ITT's CEO was the first time a search consultant's involvement in the recruiting process was highly publicized. That a search consultant was involved in such a major CEO search and that this was an excellent hire for ITT combined to legitimize search consultants as part of the process.

Still, it took many years before search consultants were routinely contracted for outside searches. Companies viewed these CEO searches with great seriousness and invested significant thought and energy in researching candidates and determining which one was uniquely qualified to meet their needs. Through the 1970s and 1980s, organizations were especially concerned about finding the right person to lead them. Because people tended to stay with organizations for a long time, and a CEO's tenure was frequently ten or twenty years, everyone wanted to make sure that the fit was perfect.

Search consultants, too, made a huge investment in time and energy. It wasn't unusual back then to research two hundred or even three hundred people for the position, narrow the list to a hundred, and then begin the process of contacting candidates by phone and letter and interviewing interested candidates several times. Client management and the search consultant would roll up their collective sleeves, analyze what the company's business needs were, and develop the specifications for the position. The search consultant would then create an initial list and pare it down to a manageable size by using the criteria they established. The people remaining on the list were researched and interviewed to the point that the client company had great insight into the candidate's strengths and weaknesses. Much time was spent telephoning resource people, asking for referrals and references. Without the benefit of the technology that exists today, searchers often had only trade association lists and *Who's Who* biographies to research candidates.

Although obtaining information about candidates was more difficult, the search for a CEO was easier in the sense that searchers were often looking within a familiar group. Until relatively recently, organizations worked hard to grow and develop their own talent and often had a pool of qualified candidates from which to choose. Even when they did go outside, however, they often knew who the candidates were and didn't have to do a global search for a successor. Senior executives from different companies often moved in the same circles; they belonged to the same country clubs if they lived in the same city or they were important members of the industry trade association. Figuratively and literally, it was a smaller world, and the majority of potential candidates for a given CEO position were often well known and targeted by the client company. Until the 1980s there were fewer and more dominant companies in a limited number of industries, thus further narrowing the field of candidates. In addition, it was easier to put together a compensation package, which consisted of base salary, bonus, and stock options. And of course, it was much more likely that when a CEO position was offered to a candidate, he would accept it. Unlike today, people (including internal candidates who were offered the top spot) didn't think about turning down the job or shopping around to see what other offers they could muster. More than one new CEO accepted the position and then simply went home and told his family that they were moving.

The impetus to go outside for a CEO was also different years ago. Typically, it would be the result of a change in strategy or direction and the recognition that no current executive had the skills to implement this strategy effectively. In many instances, the organization would have brought in a consulting firm that designed a new structure or strategy. This design would mandate new leadership, and the company would look outward for that leader. A search consultant would then be retained. (In fact, early in my career, I obtained many of my clients via referrals from strategic consulting firms.)

In looking back, I'm not calling for a return to the "good old days." In certain ways, we're much smarter today about how we go about selecting CEOs. We have information technology that helps us research candidates' backgrounds with ease and speed; boards are much more willing to consider a diverse group of candidates rather than members of the "club"; and companies don't automatically decide to hire an insider because they're convinced an outside candidate wouldn't fit in. However, I'm disturbed by the lack of diligence, effort, and analysis that sometimes marks CEO searches. I've seen searches in which boards did cursory interviews with candidates. I know of search firms that relied on a "canned" list of candidates rather than develop one specifically for a company's requirements. I've witnessed searches in which no one bothered to get the specifications right. And on top of this, the reason some companies decide to look outside for their CEO candidates is that they haven't bothered to develop an executive pipeline or implement their own management succession plan.

In other words, much more insight and hard work used to go into the CEO selection and succession processes. Just as alarming, incumbent CEOs are much more likely to impose their will on the process and unbalance the selection decision. Given that the selection of a CEO is now more important than ever before, these flaws are scary. They are a large part of why the CEO failure rate is at an all-time high.

Straight Talk

One of the themes that you'll find running through this book is my insistence on straight talk. The lack of open, honest communication among selectors is often a contributing factor to poor selection decisions. Time and again, I've seen boards unwilling to tell a powerful CEO that his choice for his successor is not the best one, or I've heard stories about search consultants who were more interested in booking and billing a search than in confronting boards that were going about the process the wrong way.

For this reason, you'll see that there's a great deal of straight talk in the following pages. I'm going to share stories with you about the searches I've been involved in as well as lessons learned. Although I will change names of certain people and companies when I feel it is appropriate, I will be brutally honest about the CEO selection failures I've witnessed (and in some cases, participated in). I have thirty-five years worth of stories to tell, and I intend to tell the ones that illuminate the sometimes dark and mysterious corners of CEO selection.

Besides the stories, you'll also find a variety of checklists, questions, and analytical tools to help you increase the effectiveness of your approaches to succession and selection. They, too, have their basis in straight talk. They're designed to facilitate analysis of everything from the willingness of a chief human resources officer (CHRO) to stand up to a CEO who is intruding on the board's territory to a candidate's willingness to ask the tough questions (and demand the answers).

The middle section of the book contains five chapters devoted to each of the players in the selection dynamic: the incumbent CEO, the board members, the executive search consultant, the CHRO, and the candidates. In these chapters, I'll look at the attitudes and actions of each group, identify dysfunctional behaviors, and suggest what people need to do to increase the odds of making wise CEO selections. In addition, a narrative opens each of these five chapters of what you might "hear" if you could read the minds of a typical dysfunctional CEO, board member, and so on. The board member, for instance, reveals how indebted he is to the incumbent CEO; he admits that he is supporting the CEO's internal choice for his successor more out of loyalty than out of the conviction that he's the right selection. These narratives are the ultimate straight talk, albeit straight talk that is rarely heard.

As you'll discover, my point isn't that these five participants in selection are inherently dishonest individuals. Most of them are highly intelligent, talented people who want to make the right selection. But somewhere along the way, their good intentions are subverted by systemic pressures and human nature. CEOs, for instance, have to have healthy egos to get the job in the first place. Healthy egos, however, can be pushed over the line toward unhealthy narcissism by pressures for short-term performance or ego-inflating media coverage. Similarly, board members can come to feel that personal loyalty to the CEO trumps their governance responsibilities. All this doesn't make them bad people but very human ones. The antidote to these mistaken beliefs is straight talk.

What You Get Out of the Book Depends on Who You Are

CEOs are going to read this book differently than CHROs will. Human resources executives will approach it with a different set of expectations than other executives. Board members will have their own special concerns. Recognizing these differences, I've tried to take a step back and view the process holistically. I have not written this book from the point of view of one search consultant to another or for board members only. Instead, I've focused on the interrelationships among all the participants. As a result, every reader should find this book relevant to his or her role and responsibilities. Specifically,

- *Board members* will gain insight about how to overcome their often unconscious leadership biases and select the candidate who best meets the strategic needs of the organization.

- *Incumbent CEOs* will be able to explore the fine line between securing the company's future and establishing their own legacies.

- *Prospective candidates* will learn about candidates' common naive assumptions and how to get past them in order to evaluate a CEO offer objectively.

- *Human resources executives* will discover how they can assume more important roles in CEO succession and selection and help the selection committee avoid common mistakes.

- *Search consultants* will find ways to increase the likelihood that their clients will select the right candidate.

In addition, I hope this book provides a general business audience with food for thought. This is an "inside baseball" type of book, offering outsiders a look at how the CEO selection process really works. For anyone who has ever wondered why the organization chose John to be CEO when they should have chosen Mary, this book will satisfy that curiosity. More than that, it will demythologize the process. People labor under countless misconceptions about how CEOs are selected. These misconceptions include: powerful executive search consultants control who is selected; strong internal candidates have no chance against external candidates of equal or even lesser ability; board members always defer to incumbent CEOs in making selection decisions.

The truth is more complicated than these simplistic misconceptions. Neither what's wrong with the current system nor its solution can be summarized in a sentence. I find the inside story fascinating. I trust that you will feel the same way, no matter what your position inside or outside an organization might be.

Finally, I've written this book for both men and women. This may seem as though I'm stating the obvious, but not too many years ago, those involved in CEO selection decisions were almost exclusively male. Fortunately, things have changed, and though we may not have achieved true equality yet, every year seems to bring more announcements of women appointed to CEO positions. What is just as significant, more women are serving on boards, becoming human resources chiefs, and establishing successful careers as executive search consultants. Given all this, I've struggled with the pronoun issue that bedevils most authors. I arrived at the less-than-perfect solution of using gender-neutral plurals as often as possible but falling back on the male pronoun in other instances. The latter decision was based on the simple fact that the majority of CEO searches I've conducted involved men. Nonetheless, I trust that women readers will understand that the advice and ideas in this book are as relevant to women as they are to men.

The Need for More Open Discussion and Debate

Although there is sometimes a legitimate need for secrecy when conducting a CEO search, the process itself should not be a secret. The power and influence consolidated in the CEO position is enormous. Because we're not doing such a good job in selecting our CEOs these days, a more open examination of the process is called for.

I hope to stimulate such a discussion through my analysis. Certainly there are other books on this topic, and many of them do a fine job of pointing out problems or offering solutions. But I suspect that this book will be more provocative. Unlike some of the other authors, I don't have an ax to grind; I do not have a full-time business to promote (though I still do some consulting to CEOs and boards) and thus I am not hamstrung by clients, partners, or business considerations. I've found that other books often overlook critical but sensitive issues. To my knowledge, no other book examines the get-it-done-quick impetus of many CEO searches—how organizations seek instant gratification and expect to identify candidates and make a selection with absurd speed (and often resulting in an absurd selection). Similarly, other books shy away from the issues of how CHROs sometimes act as the CEO's henchman by attempting to control the search consultant and steer his efforts in a very specific direction. And few books have the temerity to focus on "retired" CEOs who are retired in name only, serve on boards, reside in corporate offices, and make it impossible for even the right CEO to be effective.

These topics need to be aired. We need more than one authorial voice raising these issues. Now, when organizations are facing the greatest challenges in their histories, we must search for and select chief executives whose skills and leadership styles are matched to their organizations' requirements. I don't expect such a small thing as a book to work miracles; organizations aren't going to change their approach to CEO selection overnight. But if I can help start a dialogue about CEO selection, I'll be satisfied. In fact, if this book simply prevents one board of directors from selecting the wrong CEO or one CEO candidate from accepting the wrong job, my mission will have been fulfilled.

July 2001   Frederick W. Wackerle
Chicago, Illinois

The Right CEO

Chapter One

Why We Need a New Process Now

Gil Amelio of Apple, Durk Jager of Procter & Gamble, Doug Ivester of Coca-Cola, Al Thoman of Xerox, John Walter of AT&T, Jill Barad of Mattel, Eckhard Pfeiffer of Compaq, and Lloyd Ward of Maytag—all these former CEOs of top corporations (or in the case of Walter, the former CEO heir apparent) share two characteristics: They are all very bright people with sterling track records as managers and leaders; they all failed as CEOs (or never got the chance to succeed).

These are not isolated cases. Every day brings stories about CEOs who left their organizations in chaos or controversy. Some had been promoted from within to the CEO position, whereas others had been recruited from the outside through extensive and expensive searches. Some left on their own, whereas others were forced out with hefty severance packages. All entered with great expectations and exited angry and frustrated. Along the way, something went terribly wrong. And it continues to go wrong in companies large and small, not only in this country but in other countries as well. For every story that makes the paper about a disturbing departure of a CEO, there are countless others that aren't reported. Despite all the selection, succession, and search processes that are in place—or perhaps because of these processes—we're choosing the wrong people to head our organizations.

Certainly poor CEO choices were also made in the past. But they weren't made with the frequency or devastating effects that are occurring today. Years ago, the environment was simpler, the strategic business issues were more straightforward, and boards had the

1

time to take long looks at internal candidates, whom they almost always selected. In the 1950s and 1960s, organizations generally found it easier to select the right CEO. But the difficulty of selecting a CEO has increased with each passing decade. Part of the problem has to do with the selection process. Given the growing complexity of the environment in which CEOs are chosen, you might think that the selection process would have evolved accordingly. It has not. In many cases, boards, incumbent CEOs, chief human resources officers (CHROs), and search consultants show less diligence and are more prone to take shortcuts than in the past. As we'll discover, the process they use is often not up to the challenge before them.

Before examining the problems this process has produced, let's focus on the current environment and how it has raised the performance bar for all CEOs.

Good Is No Longer Good Enough

It used to be an easier, more forgiving job. Until relatively recently—say ten or fifteen years ago—chief executives were better trained, had broader experience, and had defined roles to play. Though they sometimes had to confront difficult issues and challenges, most chief executives had both the power and time necessary to deal with these issues and challenges. It was unusual for a CEO to be driven from office or to resign in disgust. There was more privacy within which to do the job and more margin for error.

All this has changed. Being a CEO today is a pressure-packed, nerve-wracking, and sometimes impossible job. The issues organizations face have grown more complex than in the past, and dealing with these issues often requires a comfort level with ambiguity and paradox. Imagine trying to name a chief executive given the following stated parameters:

> We need to find someone who can help us make the transition to e-commerce. For years, we've been dragging our heels, and now our

competition has a significant edge in this area. The problem is that there's a lot of politics going on; there's a lot of resistance in the company to shifting time, energy, and resources away from our traditional distribution channels and toward the Internet. People in our sales groups, especially, feel threatened by e-commerce, and the former CEO came up through the sales ranks and intends to remain active on the board after his successor takes over.

Our company has always had a gentlemanly culture, and it's fair to say that we have studiously avoided conflict and confrontation over the years. Unfortunately, we no longer occupy the market leadership position we once did and need to get rid of deadwood and raise performance levels across the board. Our new CEO is going to have to take some tough actions that veteran employees are going to view in a harsh light. In fact, they will probably complain that the new CEO is not "one of our kind of people," though in fact we need a CEO who is not one of our kind.

We're not sure what kind of chief executive officer we require. On one hand, we'd like someone who can carry on the tradition this company has established and who will display the same qualities and competencies as the previous CEO, who held the position for eighteen years. On the other hand, we realize our pyramid structure is outdated and that we haven't taken risks by investing in new technologies, and this is starting to hurt our overall performance and our product quality. So we're kind of caught in the middle in terms of what direction to take, and we're hoping the new CEO will help us create a viable strategy that upholds our tradition yet makes some changes.

These scenarios only begin to suggest how difficult—and how essential—it is to find the right candidate for the job. More so than ever before, organizations must get the CEO specifications right. The specs, however, are no longer the same or similar for every CEO position. Organizations are facing highly individualized problems and opportunities, and as a result need very specific types of leaders at the top. One company may need to grapple with diversity issues, while another requires a visionary who can imagine a future for the company that has little to do with its past. One organization may need to find someone who feels comfortable in a newly flattened structure, while another may seek an individual who is capable of thinking and planning on a global basis.

Given the pace of change, the pressure for short-term performance, the information revolution, the demands of e-commerce, the global marketplace, team-based structures, and scores of other developments, companies no longer have the luxury of hiring merely competent chief executives. There are too many complex issues that demand immediate and effective attention. To hope that a moderately qualified candidate will grow into the job is a dangerous gamble. To make the perfect match between an organization's needs and a candidate's expertise and experience—and to make the match with all due speed—is crucial.

The current system doesn't achieve this goal. Let's look at what's broken in our current search, succession, and selection processes and why it needs to be fixed immediately.

The Five-Headed Monster

Consider the delicate dynamic among the incumbent CEO, the CEO candidates, the board members, the CHRO, and the executive search consultant. These five people or groups all play a role in choosing the next CEO. It's a delicate dynamic because if even one of these five isn't playing their role effectively, the wrong person is likely to be chosen for the job. Increasingly, this dynamic is dysfunctional. One or more of the participants refuses to accept reality, and a psychologist might say that these people are in denial about some aspect of the organization and their role in it. Historically, this has not always been the case. Years ago, our five participants tended not to make the selection mistakes that are commonly made today because they generally were more realistic about what they needed to do to select the right CEO and more serious about their roles as part of the process. Though the process back then was far from perfect—it suffered from an overreliance on the old boys' network, for instance—it often produced a CEO who was well-suited for the job.

As we look at the dysfunctional elements of our five process participants, therefore, we'll also examine how these dysfunctions have emerged historically.

Chief Executive Officer

Until relatively recently, most chief executives took the issue of their succession very seriously and attempted to groom candidates to succeed them. Often, they chose from among senior executives who had been with the company for twenty years and had been rotated among seven or eight significant business-intensive positions so that each of them was prepared for the job. Although these CEOs also tended to discriminate against all sorts of candidates—women, minorities, job-jumpers, the young, people who didn't go to the right schools, and so on—they usually trained their successors well. Unfortunately, many chief executives today don't place the same emphasis on developing their successors internally.

Perhaps that's because they don't want to think about anyone replacing them, a thought that was not quite as irksome to CEOs in the past. As "royalty," they were expected to pass their kingdom on to an appropriate "heir." Until the 1990s, many CEOs were monarchs of mahogany row. Entering their offices, one had to pass through various checkpoints and rooms until finally arriving at their sanctuary. Typically, a reception area and an anteroom with the CEO's executive secretary guarding a closed door had to be traversed. The office itself was grand, usually on the top floor, and filled with everything from a private bar to expensive artwork. Robert Lear, a former CEO and Columbia Business School professor, captures the old CEO gestalt well in an article published on the Internet [www.chiefexecutive.net] (June 2000). He suggests that years ago, they were "proud members of the CEO Club" and that they "obeyed the unwritten rules of its exclusive franchise." Lear doesn't simply disparage this exclusive mind-set but also explains a positive side to it: "But the old CEO Club did stand for some pretty good things. A certain dignity of office. An increasing adherence to better codes of ethics and improving corporate governance."

Though today's CEO still has a strong ego, he's likely to have that ego shaken by criticism and controversy. Today, the CEO's time in office is shorter, and whatever he builds is likely to change or be torn down much more quickly. That's why many CEOs often focus on the legacy they'll leave and look to hire a successor who will preserve their legacy and preserve and extend what they've created—and why retired CEOs often hang around for years, maintaining an office in the building and serving on the board. Procter & Gamble, for instance, allowed two previous CEOs to maintain their offices at P&G headquarters. But having two former chief executives hovering over the shoulder of the current CEO strikes me as a dysfunctional arrangement.

Today's CEOs receive such enormous salaries and benefits packages and their actions are reported so extensively by the media that they almost can't help but believe their press clippings and overestimate their own importance. As a result, they harm the selection dynamic in three ways.

First, they often move agonizingly slowly when facing succession issues. Even though their board is telling them it's time for them to face this issue and they've agreed with the board, they don't have any sense of urgency (even when there is a real business urgency to find their replacement). They worry about a loss of identity when they're no longer an enterprise leader, and they do everything possible to delay that from happening. There are chief executives who while publicly bemoaning their company's failure to find an internal successor have privately been happy about this failure; it confirms for them that no one can take their place, that their skills and vision are unique.

Second, some CEOs search for replacements who are mirror

images of themselves. Whether consciously or unconsciously, they don't look for the best candidate but for one who will "carry on my legacy." Typically, that's either an internal protégé or someone from the outside who thinks and acts like they do.

Third, we've all observed chief executives who simply take their eye off the ball. In their final months (or even years) on the job, their focus is on retirement dates and packages rather than on finding the right person for the organization's well-being. I know of more than one CEO who was more concerned about maintaining his use of the company jet after retirement than working on succession planning.

Boards

Board members unbalance the selection dynamic through a rubber stamp mentality and insufficient knowledge about CEO requirements. This dysfunctional behavior, too, has its roots in the past. Years ago, boards were much less involved in governance and CEO succession issues. To a certain extent, they were less involved simply because there were fewer CEO searches conducted than there are today. But it was also because of the board mentality that existed for years, a mentality that disdained the outside world. Boards used to be joined at the hip with the CEO, and they pretty much followed his lead in all things, especially the choice of his successor. That isn't to say that boards didn't participate in the succession process years ago, but that their participation was often nothing more than a formality. In some instances, they might contract with a search consultant to look for outside candidates, all the while knowing that the CEO was going to select an internal person for the job.

Now boards have become much more involved in governance and succession, and they're expected to lead the CEO search process. Because of the diversity of a board's composition, legal concerns, and the fact that they may serve the company longer than the CEO, they often take their responsibilities more seriously than boards in the past. Nonetheless, the tradition of board members being cronies of the CEO hasn't disappeared, and boards often are reluctant to challenge a CEO, especially a powerful and successful one. They feel obligated to the incumbent for naming them to the board and often have strong social ties to the CEO. For these reasons, they may well rubber stamp a CEO's selection.

In addition, many board members are simply too busy to spend the time required to make the right selection. It's very difficult these days to convince a board member to volunteer to head the CEO selection committee. Some simply don't want to make the investment in time or deal with the headaches. Others are too closely tied to the CEO and don't want to step on his toes. Most are neophytes when it comes down to conducting an external CEO search.

Part of the problem, too, is that board members don't know their organizations as well as they should. If you were to ask a given board member to explain his company's strategies and its vision for the future, he would probably not be up to the task. As a result, boards often search for candidates without knowing what they should be looking for. If they don't know that the company must switch directions over the next five years and become more technologically driven, they may fail to look for a candidate with this strength. In reality, strategic goals and visions are more complex than the preceding example, and board members need to understand the complexities in order to evaluate candidates properly.

On more than one occasion, board members have told me, "I really don't know what kind of CEO we need," or words to that effect. This is a terribly sad, terribly embarrassing admission, yet most of these board members confessed it with a shrug.

Finally, and perhaps most significantly, many boards are aging. Though there certainly are exceptions, board members in their seventies often are more concerned with the company's present than its future. In addition, older boards tend to have business philosophical differences with incoming CEOs and other top executives, who often are at least twenty years younger. Not only are they sometimes skeptical of the new business ideas of a younger generation, but also they often don't give a new CEO a fair chance; they're much quicker to criticize a fifty-something chief executive than their contemporary who appointed them to the board in the first place.

As you can see, boards can throw off the selection dynamic in all sorts of ways. Here are some of the more common actions and attitudes that cause problems:

- Confining a search to internal candidates for the wrong reasons
- Confining a search to external candidates for the wrong reasons
- Selecting the wrong search consultants
- Failing to implement a board-supervised executive pipeline process
- Failing to recognize the lack of a CEO heir apparent
- Failing to assess whether a CEO is stale, a caretaker, or whether he should be replaced
- Being ignorant of how the company compares when benchmarked against competitors, the loyalty of employees, the depth of executive talent

CEO Candidates

Executives used to be willing to wait their turn. The unwritten rule in most organizations was that if you put in your time and displayed loyalty to the company and competence in your job, you would be rewarded. It might take thirty years of waiting, but eventually you would at least have a decent chance of being selected if you played your cards right; it was your job to lose. They knew that the odds were against the company passing over qualified internal candidates and finding someone from another industry (or someone younger, or a woman). In fact, I remember many candidates being offended when we (search consultants) approached them about a CEO position. They resented the implication that we thought they'd be willing to "desert" their companies. Most candidates also had been mentored to succeed within a very specific corporate culture and assumed that they would have difficulty doing well in other cultures. Others weren't interested because of loyalty to their companies, their people, and their bosses.

Today, in the absence of selection rules, long-term employment by one company, and two-way loyalty, CEO candidates tend to upset the delicate balance of the selection process with their naiveté. In countless interviews, I've met candidates who accepted the CEO-successor job without ever coming to terms with whether they have the skills and knowledge an organization requires or whether they are a good match for the culture. They're so anxious to become CEO and leave their current organization that they don't squarely confront the reality of the new position. Similarly, they're willing to accept whatever conditions the incumbent CEO sets down, even though they may place unacceptable limits on their ability to set direction for the enterprise. Or even more troubling, they believe the CEO when he tells them that even though he's going to remain with the company for the next five years and sit on his hand-picked board, he will never interfere.

To a certain extent, candidates are victims of a system that does a poor job of preparing them to be CEO. Today, relatively few senior executives have had a pure profit-and-loss (P&L) experience. With a matrix structure or functional management style, companies aren't preparing people to run the whole show. There aren't many executives with direct reporting responsibilities to the CEO, a situation that prevents the on-the-job learning that prepares people for the top spot. In addition, downsizing cuts a wide swath, and many potential candidates have either been physically removed from a company's talent pool or they've been sufficiently disillusioned that they have no interest in working for a large company again in any capacity.

A related issue is the lack of solid leadership development programs in companies. Finding internal candidates can be difficult if the leadership cupboard is bare. Too many organizations spend the bulk of their development dollars helping people learn specific jobs and skills and give short shrift to growing their own leaders. Consequently, companies find they lack the visionaries, strategists, risk-takers, and big thinkers needed for the CEO position. Because of this lack, they are forced to look at outside candidates who may be qualified to be CEOs but are unfamiliar with a company's culture or goals. These candidates are in for a shock when they accept the CEO position and find out very quickly that their leadership style and skills clash with the gestalt of their new companies.

Into this environment enter native candidates who are taken in by an egotistical CEO's song-and-dance about how he won't interfere or who actually believe that they can win over a skeptical board. Sometimes, they accept without question the board's or CEO's description of the company's financial and strategic positions, never realizing that they've been fed a sugar-coated version of reality. This naiveté doesn't just get these candidates in trouble; it causes a company to spend months or years in limbo as the candidates accept the job and then leave shortly thereafter when they realize they were deceived.

Search Consultants

Search consultants used to conduct much more thorough searches than are done today. By "thorough," I mean that more candidates were interviewed more times, and a greater effort was made prior to conducting the search to understand a given organization's business goals and strategies and how each potential candidate might help achieve them. Boards respected this effort because it fulfilled their mission of due diligence. Incumbent CEOs thought it appropriate because it helped them locate the individual who was best capable of maintaining (and sometimes building upon) what the incumbent had created. Most of the major search consultants routinely did their homework; they invested the time and energy necessary to sort through many candidates and find the perfect match between company and individual. Most organizations accepted that consultants could not find suitable candidates unless they diligently researched the company and the candidates, and they accepted that this would be a time-consuming process.

In the past, search consultants were trained as management consultants, and they brought a strong business and strategic mentality to the table. Executive search consultants came out of A. T. Kearney, Booz Allen & Hamilton , McKinsey, and George Fry, and these consultants were attuned to the issues facing CEOs and boards. They established a true partnership with their clients, and both the search consultants and their clients expected objective and detailed feedback. Back then, a search consultant would have been insulted to be called a headhunter and would have resented the implications that he was a mercenary out for a quick kill.

Today, search consultants sometimes lack business training and willingness to do in-depth research and interviewing. CHROs, CEOs, and boards put pressure on them to find someone quickly (and sometimes cheaply), and they respond to this pressure by "transacting" the search and even approach executives in client companies. A common transactional tactic involves recycling the same old names for different positions. Most search firms keep a "bin" of candidate résumés that they present to their previous clients, and when they book a new search, they look through the bin to see whether there are any names that might be acceptable to the new client. Although search firms often feel that this bin is their competitive advantage, it is nothing more than a lazy consultant's time-saving device that yields generic candidates. Unique research is required to find a CEO. In other words, the unique requirements of the company must be identified and a wide net must be cast to find the few people who match these requirements. This means going beyond the standard list of names and being creative in the search; it requires a search consultant to make a lot of calls and ask a lot of people whether they know anyone who might fit the requirements like a glove. This type of research used to be standard practice in the search industry, but today it is the exception rather than the rule. It has been delegated to "back-room" people who have little exposure to clients or candidates.

Certainly there are excellent search firms out there today, but the increase in firms who fit the headhunter description is distressing. It takes knowledge, effort, and resourcefulness to fill a CEO position, and when any or all of these traits are absent in a search, the result is often an inappropriate candidate. Remember, only 4 percent of total searches are CEO searches, meaning that a very small percentage of search consultants have had the experience to conduct these critical assignments properly.

Heads of Human Resources

Before the term *human resources* ever existed, there were personnel heads and managers of labor or industrial relations. Back then, personnel had nothing to do with selecting or searching for a CEO.

Theoretically, HR chiefs today should play a pivotal role in helping organizations identify, develop, and select the right potential CEOs from within. More than anyone else in organizations, they know what type of talent is needed. From a human asset standpoint, they know what their companies need and what they have in abundance. They also are skilled at defining the job specifications; they can translate the requirements articulated by board members and the incumbent CEO into job specs that can be used internally or by a search firm.

Many HR chiefs today do participate on CEO succession teams. In fact, my firm conducted a survey of 350 chief HR officers and found that only 6.6 percent of those surveyed said they had no role in CEO successor selection, whereas almost 68 percent said that they were more involved in successor searches than in the past. What is surprising, almost 78 percent of respondents said they were involved in CEO, COO, or board searches. A number of factors accounted for this increased participation, ranging from having closer relationships with the incumbent CEO to being included as an active member of the senior executive team.

Although HR chiefs do have a more active role in the succession process than in the past, this role is often limited. Sometimes HR heads serve as henchmen for the incumbent CEO, acting as a liaison between the organization and an executive search consulting firm. Or they do some preliminary interviewing or administrative tasks connected to the CEO search. Rarely, however, are they made primary partners in the process and their specific skills and resources—knowledge of the company's internal people, psychological insights, and contacts with executive search consultants—aren't maximized.

When HR heads are excluded from the business process or their roles are demeaned, the company loses a valuable perspective and resource. The unfortunate attitude of many organizations is that the leadership development process is not a strategic business process. In fact, that's exactly what it is.

How an Unbalanced Dynamic Is Producing Ill-Matched CEOs

Creating the right specs for any CEO position requires hard work and insight. There are many subtleties and complexities that need to be factored into the equation, and a team effort is required to capture these subtleties and complexities. Just as important, there needs to be a series of checks and balances along the way to ensure that one person's opinion about the position—usually the incumbent CEO's opinion—doesn't overwhelm all other considerations. On a number of occasions, I've seen strong CEOs push their handpicked successor on the company, or dominate boards and prevent them from orchestrating the process, or mislead CEO candidates who shortly thereafter quit in disgust. Sometimes these chief executive officers have the best of intentions; they truly believe that they know what's best for their organizations. But even if they're sincere in these beliefs, their dominance skews the process and results in a flawed selection or a situation that dooms the new CEO to failure.

Similarly, boards need to be alert for CEOs who have not provided for their succession; this is sign that the CEO might be dysfunctional and will often throw off the selection dynamic. Companies with strong succession plans often have strong business results. It's no coincidence that General Electric has made leadership succession a top priority. Without a succession plan, the search is artificially tipped toward external candidates.

Organizations need to rebalance this unbalanced dynamic. If they don't, they'll end up in situations similar to those that confronted the following companies.

The Overreactive Board

With hindsight, Apple's decision to name Gil Amelio CEO was a major blunder that continues to haunt the company. In his autobiographical account of the event, Amelio clearly communicates how his decision to take on the job was ultimately a mistake. After Apple's board helped send cofounder and CEO Steven Jobs packing, Amelio, an Apple board member, took on the job himself. On the surface, it may have made sense to Amelio and the board. He was a smart, successful former chief executive who knew about Apple's problems from serving on the board. Despite his smarts and his talent, however, he was the wrong person for the job. He had little understanding of Apple's culture. Actually, though he may have understood the culture intellectually, he lacked an emotional identification with that culture and a grasp of how important the culture was for both the people who worked at Apple and the organization's success. Amelio's tenure was marked by false starts and product mistakes, and the company lost a great deal of momentum. Though the board did induce Jobs to return and Apple's fortunes have picked up, they came perilously close to the edge.

Boards that overreact is one of the unbalancing factors in this day and age. For a highly public company such as Apple that receives significant media and financial analyst scrutiny, board overreaction is an omnipresent danger. Although it may be an overstatement to say that Apple's board panicked, they certainly responded to the pressure they were feeling from various stakeholders. They lost sight of Apple's culture and never established CEO candidate qualifications that fit that culture.

Search Firms That Work from Bad Information

Another unbalancing factor involves search firms that are working from bad information. Years ago, it was almost inconceivable that a CEO or board would provide a search firm with inaccurate information about an organization's needs or future direction. Today it's all too common. For instance, the CEO of a large manufacturing company informed his board that he intended to retire within the year, and the board began the search for his successor. The CEO had met with the board and briefed them about the state of the business, clearly communicating that the company's superior technology and product quality would stand them in good stead for years to come. In fact, he had stated outright that they were the premier low-cost manufacturer in their industry, not mentioning that they also had some of the highest labor rates. The CEO's only concerns—and he emphasized they were relatively minor ones— involved motivating their dealer network and getting the sales force better organized. As a result, the board brought in a search firm and instructed them to look for a CEO with strong sales, marketing, and dealership experience.

What the board didn't know, because the incumbent CEO didn't tell them, was that the company was in great need of a fast turnaround. Serious cost and quality issues had recently surfaced that the CEO had hidden from the board out of vanity; he foolishly hoped that these issues would resolve themselves on their own. This enterprise leader was so worried about his legacy and fearful of any blot on his record that he convinced himself that this wasn't an issue that would impact choosing a new CEO.

The CEO wasn't the only culpable party in this crime. The board had no process in place to question the CEO about organizational needs or assess his answers. To make matters worse, they had a well-crafted consultant analysis secreted away in the CEO's desk drawer. If they had been privy to this analysis or had a CEO assessment process in place, they would have asked him the type of tough questions that would have forced his hand. Instead, in typical board fashion, they flew in on the day of the meeting, had a few quick committee meetings, and enjoyed a nice lunch. After the meal, everyone started looking at their watches and were grateful to get out of there as quickly as possible. The HR chief, too, who might have been able to identify this crying organizational need, was excluded from the committee's search process. The sales-and-marketing-oriented CEO they eventually hired was completely incapable of creating the fast turnaround the company desperately needed, and the desperate straits they found themselves in shortly thereafter made them a prime target of a corporate raider. Despite downsizing and other measures, the company is still in trouble.

The process is unbalanced by a combination of factors: CEOs who are more worried about their legacies than the company's future, boards that lack a formal procedure for evaluating CEO candidate requirements, and HR executives who are absent from the process. If any one of these groups had fulfilled their proper role, some balance would have been restored and an appropriate CEO might have been hired. As it was, the search consultant was operating with erroneous information. This is a true story; it happened to me.

The Starstruck Board

Another unbalancing factor is a starstruck board—a board that believes talent can cure anything that ails the organization. Rather than doing their homework and pinning down the specific traits, competencies, and experiences appropriate for CEO candidates, they look for miracle men and women. Because we live in an era in which certain CEOs have been turned into celebrities by the media, it's only natural that some boards have been seduced by certain CEOs' mystiques. Even when the mystique is earned—when it's based on savvy judgment and spectacular results—it shouldn't substitute for analysis of what a company really needs.

Sunbeam, for instance, was seduced by Al Dunlap. Dunlap's radical cost-cutting techniques had resulted in turnarounds at Scott Paper and other companies. His star was shining bright when Sunbeam's board offered him the position. As it turned out, his techniques were ineffective at Sunbeam and his ineffectiveness (not to mention the enmity his Draconian measures created) eventually cost him his job. If Sunbeam's board had simply determined the five or six qualities they needed in a CEO and the leadership style that fit the company, they probably wouldn't have hired Dunlap.

The "Grass Is Always Greener" Syndrome

The fourth unbalancing factor involves the "grass is always greener" syndrome. Some organizations steadfastly believe that it's better to bring in an outsider as CEO rather than choose someone internally. There are times when it makes sense to recruit an outsider; some organizations need to be shaken up and require fresh blood. Increasingly, however, we're seeing companies spending enormous amounts of time and money on searches, scouring the planet for a savior. More so than ever before, an outside search seems like standard operating procedure. When inside candidates are automatically ignored, potentially outstanding candidates are not even considered. All other things being equal, the inside candidate at least is familiar with the culture and business, a trait that gives him a leg up on outside candidates.

One need look no further than Hewlett-Packard to see the changes that have taken place in CEO selection. It used to be impossible to recruit any top executives away from Hewlett-Packard; they had a wealth of talent and wouldn't have considered looking elsewhere for their CEO. Recently, however, they brought in Carly Fiorina as their new CEO, offering her a reported total compensation package approaching $90 million. Perhaps it is worth it. But it's also worth considering whether such an expenditure of money and effort was necessary, and whether stockholders' money might have been better spent in other ways.

Although some CEOs from the outside can come into a company, rally the troops, and create a sense of followership, others arrive and are immediately overwhelmed by what they need to learn. Rather than being highly visible and engaged leaders, they lock themselves in with a few key executives and mounds of data. Because they don't spend enough time with key customers, employees, and other significant stakeholders, they are always viewed as outsiders.

Therefore, organizations need to analyze what type of leader an outside CEO will be, and ask the questions and do the analysis necessary to make sure he becomes one who can rally the troops.

Analyzing Your Own CEO Selection Process

Given the shorter tenure of CEOs in today's volatile environment, it's likely that most companies will need to replace their top people relatively frequently. Successful CEOs are hotly recruited and will be sorely tempted by spectacular offers from other organizations. Unsuccessful ones will leave even faster. And even moderately successful chief executives can burn out quickly. Not only are they under intense media scrutiny, but they also have to deal with the pressures of dissident shareholder groups, pension fund management issues, and growing corporate governance.

Given these pressures, every company should have a sense of how effective their CEO selection, succession, and search processes have been or might be. To give you this sense, answer the following questions:

1. Was your company's most recent choice of a CEO a wise one?

2. If you were to replace your CEO, would the best possible candidate be inside or outside your company?

3. Does your CEO possess an ego that would make it difficult for him to work with a successor during the transition period?

4. Is the chairman of your board's search or selection committee an independent director?

5. If you were selected to lead a board search committee, would you be willing to devote time to this effort?

6. Is the CEO involved in the search engagement?

7. Has the full board signed off on the specs and the candidate profile for the new CEO?

8. Has the board structured a timetable for the CEO's transition and departure?

9. Will the retiring CEO remain on the board?

10. Is your CHRO an active and important participant in the management group?

11. Is your CHRO so close to the CEO that it's impossible for him to be objective about a successor?

12. What is your search consultant's or firm's track record for conducting searches for CEO positions similar to your own?

13. What companies is the search consultant or firm prohibited from taking employees away from?

14. How well does the search consultant or firm know your company?

15. How many other CEO searches is the consultant or firm conducting?

16. What are your company's strengths and weaknesses and what are the competitive threats; has all this been factored into the candidate specs?

17. What is your procedure for considering internal candidates (or do you not plan to consider them)?

18. Do you plan to conduct a horse race (pitting internal candidates against each other and evaluating how they perform over a given period)?

19. Is your CHRO knowledgeable and fully qualified to partici-pate in your CEO search?

20. Do you have a contingency plan to replace your CEO if he should depart unexpectedly?

21. Have you called in a CEO compensation expert to brief the board on compensation packages prior to conducting your search?

The odds are that at least some of these questions disturb you, especially if you're a CEO, CHRO, board member, search consul-tant, or CEO candidate. You may even feel threatened by some of the questions. I do not mean to be threatening, but I am intent on provoking people to confront difficult issues. If you're a board mem-ber, for instance, you may want to avoid dealing with the CEO's desire to serve on the board after he retires. This is a touchy issue, especially if you have a good relationship with your CEO. Ignoring this issue now may avoid problems in the short term but create much more serious problems in the long term.

Other questions may make you angry because they lead you to believe that a fellow participant in the selection process will sabo-tage it. For instance, you look at the questions about search firms and suspect that the search firm's book-and-bill mentality will pre-vent them from evaluating candidates thoroughly and insightfully. Or you try to answer one of the board questions and realize that the board lacks the interest, methodology, and objectivity necessary to conduct an effective CEO search.

To feel comfortable with the answers to these questions, a new process is necessary. Actually, what's really needed is an old process retooled for our current environment, as the next chapter will demonstrate.

Chapter Two

When the Right Person Is Chosen by the Right People at the Right Time

My Blue Chip Search

Over the years, I've seen the CEO selection process function almost perfectly on a number of occasions. Unfortunately, those occasions were in a past more distant than recent. One reason for this is that we used to live in simpler times, and there weren't as many complicating factors (e-commerce, the war for talent, for instance) impacting the search. But another reason has been a process breakdown, caused by stress fractures ranging from board members who aren't diligent about building leadership bench strength to the overinflated egos of incumbent CEOs to the book-and-bill mentality of search firms.

It's amazing, therefore, that some companies still manage to get it right. Despite all the obstacles, organizations pluck ideal candidates from the vine and secure leaders whose experience and expertise perfectly match their organizations' present and future needs.

It's instructive to look at these ideal scenarios. From them we can glimpse what is possible and can create a theory of the case. Certain actions and attitudes that resulted in the correct selection can be identified and formalized into a process—a process that will be described in ensuing chapters.

For now, let's focus on one search that began in 1998 and with which I was involved. Of all the searches I've done in the past thirty-five odd years, this was one where almost everything clicked and all the potential disasters (of which there were several) were avoided.

A Mutual Undertaking

Tom Wheeler, CEO and chairman of MassMutual Life Insurance Company, called me in November 1997, explaining that he wanted me to help him conduct a search for his replacement. He said that he didn't think any of his internal people were ready to take on the CEO position due to changing dynamics in the insurance industry that might threaten MassMutual's ownership structure. (Several mutually owned companies were moving toward public stock ownership.) Tom stated that he was ready to leave by the end of 1999, and now was the time to begin a search.

These types of calls are made all the time by outgoing CEOs to search consultants and search firms. The typical response is to start the search immediately. Although there are instances when speed is crucial, too often search firms rush in where fools fear to tread. The book-and-bill mentality prompts search people to sign up the client and move forward rather than helping the CEO determine whether the company is ready to begin a search.

Right Idea Number 1

Before beginning a search, clearly define the candidate profile and the business strategy, and get the board involved.

When I began asking Tom about why his internal people weren't qualified, it became clear to both of us that he was relying more on instinct than hard data. He talked in vague terms about how they didn't possess "the right strategic level" or "leadership power." Though his instincts might have been right, Tom needed to do a bit more homework before moving forward. Three danger signs loomed large after our initial conversation:

- Tom couldn't clearly describe his successor in terms of a candidate profile.
- A big question mark hovered over the future direction of the company.

- Board members hadn't discussed or provided input about the search, company strategy, or candidate specification.

After a bit of discussion, Tom agreed that he still had some homework to do and said that he would get back to me once he had done it. To help him, I suggested that he find a way to assess his inside people and determine whether they were viable candidates. By making this effort, he would also end up with a candidate profile for his successor.

Over the next few months, Tom worked with Delta Consulting and myself to create a matrix for a candidate profile. The outcome of Delta's work was the creation of a CEO candidate checklist containing twenty-seven metrics. After informing the board of his desire to step down, he appointed three board members to a CEO selection committee. They also contributed to the matrix, which settled on the following five must-have criteria:

- *Track record*. Has a record of achievement that demonstrates success in leading in a dynamic, volatile environment; experience should include successful acquisition and related integration or culture shifts; gets things done; capable of leading a large, complex business on day one.
- *Seasoned judgment*. Makes good strategic choices—knows when to emphasize and balance the organization's long-term, strategic objectives; applies broad knowledge and experience when addressing complex issues; defines and communicates strategic issues and goals clearly, despite ambiguity; makes timely, tough decisions; possesses great balance among operating systems improvement, cost, *and* top line marketing achievements.
- *Visionary thinking*. Has a vision for the business; has international perspective; maintains a long-term, big-picture view; anticipates obstacles and opportunities; generates breakthrough ideas; is an integrative thinker; develops options and sets corporate direction; willing to entertain alternative corporate

structures and governance models to achieve strategic objectives; excellent presenter to board of directors.

- *Leadership.* Plays a variety of leadership roles (for example, driving, delegating, supporting, empowering, collaborating, and coaching) as appropriate; inspires others to perform at their best; creates a climate that fosters personal investment and excellence; sets and pursues aggressive goals; drives for results; gives people opportunity and latitude to grow and achieve; high-energy type who can change a culture.

- *Personal integrity.* Does what is right for customers; role models consistency between words and actions; word is bond; establishes open, candid, trusting relationships; treats all individuals fairly and with respect; makes decisions that are effective rather than politically expedient.

Once we all had agreed on the criteria, it became apparent that Tom's instincts were right. The internal people simply didn't fit the profile. As talented as many of them were, they lacked the types of experience or skills that the company would require in the coming years. Instead of deluding his top people into thinking that they might be his successor, Tom was now able to explain to them in very specific terms why they didn't fit the profile. Right from the start, he made it clear that they weren't candidates and was very honest and open about why this was the case. He wisely avoided the trap of asking a search consultant to interview internal people to make them feel good that they're being considered for the top job even though everyone knows they're not candidates. As a result, he didn't encounter the morale problems that often beset companies when they go outside for a new CEO and internal people feel as though they were misled into believing they had a real shot at the job. In addition, when the candidate specs are made clear to internal people, they are more likely to appreciate why an outsider was chosen, since this person fits the initial candidate profile. Tom's people handled the decision to go outside very well, especially after they saw who was selected.

Right Idea Number 2

Be honest and up-front with internal people about whether they're viable CEO candidates (and if they're not, tell them why they're not).

In March, Tom called me and said they were ready to begin the search. He had obtained board buy-in for the type of person they needed, and his chief HR officer, Susan Alfano, also had become part of the process and would fulfill a meaningful role as administrator during the search. (Later in the search, Susan worked with an outside consultant to structure a compensation package for our CEO choice. This was critical, since the company lacked such a compensation package in place and needed a sophisticated plan that would be appropriate for the selected individual.)

I should make it clear from the start that this wasn't an easy or simple search. Perhaps the most significant complicating issue was the company's direction. MassMutual was a mutually owned company (owned by its policyholders). The board was conflicted as to whether it should continue to be mutually owned or become a stock company. Because there was ample and recent precedent for mutual companies successfully making the transition to stock status, some board members strongly believed this was a feasible strategy. Others relished the culture of a mutually owned company and wanted to continue that tradition. That it was an unusually large board of twenty directors—a number of new board members had been added with the company's recent acquisition of Connecticut Mutual—didn't help matters.

Perhaps the biggest asset we had in the search was a psychologically healthy CEO. Too often, incumbent CEOs consciously or unconsciously sabotage the search for their successors. They insist on finding a clone or they look for someone who they know they can manipulate. Their egos and insecurities shape the process. Tom Wheeler, however, had a refreshingly healthy approach. He'd started out as a general agent and worked his way up. As dedicated as he was to the company and as much as he loved its culture, he also recognized that the company would have to change to continue to be successful; he was willing to find a successor who had a leadership style and background very different from his own.

Unlike some CEOs, Tom wasn't threatened by the notion of having someone reinvent his company and negate some of his programs and policies. He was ready to walk away cleanly. Some CEOs hang on to their positions for dear life, whereas others can't wait to get out and thus fail at their due diligence responsibilities. Tom looked at the person who would succeed him as a partner. His plan was to create a transitional partnership that would last six to eight months, and then he would leave the company.

The three-person selection committee on the board was appropriately diverse. The chairman of the committee, Roger Ackerman, was the chairman of Corning and had experienced the phenomenon of becoming a CEO successor; Sheldon Lubar, chairman of Lubar & Co., was an entrepreneurial owner steeped in knowledge about insurance companies; John Maypole was an entrepreneurial holding company investment executive. All three knew the company well (they were long-time board members) and were independent thinkers. The composition of the committee helped guard against a bias toward a certain type of CEO. If all the members were from public companies, for instance, they may have favored a new CEO with the same background and bias.

When I first began meeting with Tom and this committee, however, I noticed that they had a tendency to defer to Tom. To a certain extent, this was understandable; Tom had been a very successful leader of the organization and they had great respect for his opinions. From a search perspective, however, it was a potential source of problems. Boards sometimes reflexively defer to the CEO, believing he is best able to make decisions about the successor. When this happens, the search process loses valuable contributors. Ideally, the board search committee will provide a greater diversity of ideas and experiences than any one individual. Even a psychologically healthy CEO such as Tom needed other voices to help make a good selection decision. To his credit, Tom recognized this fact. For this reason, he would sometimes say to his search committee when they seemed to be deferring to him, "I'm going to leave the room, and I want you meet with Fred without me around."

Right Idea Number 3

Give the board opportunities to voice opinions without interference from the CEO.

CEO searches take place for good or bad reasons, and MassMutual's was generally for a good reason. By "good," I mean that the organization was in excellent shape and there was no need to find a savior CEO. Bad reasons are when companies are in bad shape and present the incoming CEO with a major challenge. The only thing bad in MassMutual's case was that they had failed to develop an internal candidate to take the company to the next level. Part of the problem was that Tom and the board didn't talk much about this issue over the years. If they had, they probably would have been better prepared internally for replacing Tom.

The next step in the process was to present our five criteria to the board and receive agreement that this is what we'd measure each candidate against.

From the start, we decided to keep the search confidential. For control purposes, we designated our client as "Blue Chip." Only my assistant, Audrey Lehmann, and my researcher, Marianne Dewey, were aware of our client's identity. Confidentiality is an increasingly difficult code to maintain in an era in which so many people leak so much to the media. Years ago, searches as a rule were confidential. It was rare to find any company even admitting that they were using an executive search firm, since to do so was tantamount to admitting failure to develop a candidate internally. Now the names of search firms are routinely printed in articles about companies looking for new CEOs, as though the companies want to communicate that they have done their due diligence by hiring a professional.

MassMutual had good reasons for wanting to keep their search confidential; the main one was that they didn't want to create anxiety and speculation during the search. Because there was a national dialogue about the future of mutual companies, they didn't want news of their search to catalyze a bunch of rumors. Confidentiality makes sense from candidates' perspective as well because they don't want their current employers to know they're up for a position at another company (a company that may be a competitor).

From a search consultant's perspective, however, this confidentiality issue presented some challenges. You're essentially approaching prospective candidates about the most important job of their career without being able to disclose who is offering the position. To overcome this problem, we decided upon the following strategy.

Our first step would be to identify CEOs, COOs, and senior executives in the insurance and financial services industries. Once we compiled this rather large list of about a hundred people, we pared it down by looking at their experience, general management capabilities, and other factors. Relying completely on public information, we created a list of sixty candidates that Tom Wheeler and I pared down to twenty who seemed to fit the specs we had created. The search committee approved our selections. I then approached each one of them via a Federal Express letter sent to their homes that outlined the opportunity to be a CEO of a major financial services company but did not disclose the client's identity. After following up with phone calls to gauge their interest, I found that about ten of them were interested in the position, and I reviewed the results with the search committee at our next progress meeting, where we determined who to disclose the company identity to and who to put on the back burner.

After informing Tom and the search committee about these candidates and securing their approval, I disclosed who the client company was and asked them if they were still interested. A few of them bowed out because they weren't comfortable working for a mutual company. The seven who remained interested received an extensive package of information about the company. I interviewed each of them and reported back to Tom and the search committee about who I felt were the leading candidates. Five candidates remained: two with insurance company backgrounds, two from the banking industry, and one with broad-based financial services experience. After I interviewed these five people, Tom and I conducted a second round of interviews with each of the five candidates. After a couple of weeks, Tom interviewed each of the five for his second time to gain answers for any questions that arose during the first round of interviews.

Right Idea Number 4

Interviewing many candidates—and some more than once—helps you get beyond the initial profile and home in on what you're really looking for.

After we completed these interviews, we sat down with the search committee, shared our impressions of each candidate, and recommended three whom they should interview. One of the committee members asked Tom who he felt was the best person for the job and whether they might forego interviewing the candidates and go with his choice. Again, the committee reflexively was deferring to Tom. Fortunately, he wouldn't allow it and requested that they do all three interviews.

I formulated a list of questions for the committee to ask the candidates, and following each interview, I required each member of the selection committee to complete candidate evaluation sheets (see Exhibit 2.1). The evaluation sheets also provided room for comments, as well four yes-or-no questions. This formalized approach was important because there already is a great deal of subjectivity to selecting a CEO, and codifying the questions lends a necessary objectivity to the endeavor. The appraisal sheets also gave us a way to objectify the process and generate meaningful discussion by the committee.

Exhibit 2.1. CEO Evaluation

Candidate _____	RATING:	5–Clearly confident
		4–Confident
		3–Seems OK
		2–Some concern
Evaluator _____		1–Serious concern
Blue Chip 365.01		0–Did not get information

Criteria	Comments	Rating
A track record of achievement, demonstrating success in leading a dynamic, volatile environment; experience should include successful acquisition and related integration or culture shifts; capable of leading a large, complex business on day one.		
Will not gamble foolishly with the assets of the corporation. Knows how to protect and "anchor" a franchise as well as project a leadership position in a highly competitive and changing financial services environment.		
Uses seasoned judgment to make sound strategic choices—knows when to emphasize and balance the organization's long-term strategic objectives; applies broad knowledge and experience when addressing complex issues; makes timely, tough decisions.		
Has demonstrated the ability to develop a vision for the business; maintains a long-term, big picture view; anticipates obstacles and opportunities; generates breakthrough ideas; is willing to entertain alternative corporate structures and governance models to achieve strategic objectives.		

Criteria	Comments	Rating
A great leader who inspires others to perform at their best; creates a climate that fosters personal investment and excellence; sets and pursues aggressive goals; a high-energy type who can change a successful culture, keep the momentum going; drives for results; promotes collaboration and teamwork.		
Strong integrity base; establishes open, candid, trusting relationships; treats all individuals fairly and with respect; makes decisions that are effective rather than politically expedient.		
Excited by the opportunity to lead MassMutual		
	Total Rating:	

Experience in the financial services industry as a leader of a substantially distributed financial services product.	Yes	No
Clear understanding of the customer, competition, and legislative environments.	Yes	No
Clear, date-certain successor to the chairman.	Yes	No
Excellent presenter to board of directors, management team, employee population, and external communities.	Yes	No
Comments:		

After we informed the three candidates that they were finalists for the job, we asked them for references. Again, the issue of keeping the search confidential came up. Because we didn't want any media coverage or industry gossip about the search, we agreed on the strategy of telling the people contacted for references that the person in question was being considered for a spot on the board of directors of a large client. After reviewing these references, the committee gathered, discussed the candidates, and chose Bob O'Connell to be Tom's successor.

Bob was a senior executive with AIG, the leading global insurance company listed on the New York Stock Exchange. Because he had previously been with New York Life, a mutual company, Bob had an ideal combination of stock and mutual experience. He'd also participated in AIG's successful overseas expansion, which was something that could be of value to MassMutual. Bob had a terrific leadership profile; he was a "tough" guy who was also a people person. During the referencing, someone described Bob in the same way that GE's Jack Welch has been described: "He has a hard head but a soft heart." In short, Bob had the right mixture of qualities to be the CEO of a solid company such as MassMutual. As familiar as he was with MassMutual's culture and as much respect as he had for it, he was also willing to challenge the traditionalists with new ideas and strategies that he thought would be in the company's best interests.

Right Idea Number 5

There are two types of candidates you want to avoid when you're trying to make a good company better: (1) the overly soft individual who is unwilling or unable to change the corporate culture or direction and (2) the marine drill sergeant who is eager to upset the culture and doesn't care who takes offense.

It's worth analyzing why MassMutual was able to avoid hiring the "wrong" candidates. When I first interviewed the entire board,

I observed a number of members who expressed strong opinions about preserving the culture; I also listened to members who felt the company needed to be far more aggressive strategically than it had been. If the selection committee had been heavily biased in favor of either point of view, they would have made a poor decision. Tom, however, recognized this danger and wisely chose the committee with an eye toward balance. Collectively, their varying perspectives created a synergy that resulted in Bob's unanimous selection.

Tom, of course, also played a crucial role in maintaining a balanced perspective. As a psychologically healthy CEO, Tom was able to subordinate his ego for the good of the company. The best evidence of this subordination was that Bob has a very different personality and leadership style from Tom. Laid back, contemplative, and gentlemanly are traits commonly attributed Tom, whereas Bob is more blunt and results-oriented. From a leadership perspective, Tom is a hands-on leader who wants everything spelled out and insists on maintaining as much control as possible; he focused the company's efforts on its traditional areas of strength. Bob, however, is a delegator who declared that no meeting should last more than ten minutes and who insists that one third of annual sales come from a newly invented business area.

In the first year, the transition has gone even better than expected. Despite their different approaches to the job, Bob and Tom have forged the partnership Tom hoped for. In fact, Bob asked Tom to remain on the board a bit longer to help with the transition. Bob and the board decided to retain the company's mutual status, and he has made a number of strategic changes and has introduced new product innovations that have helped the company grow in new and profitable directions.

Striving for Balance

In looking back at the MassMutual CEO search, the word *balance* keeps coming up. In all the ideal or close-to-ideal searches I've been involved with, a formal system of checks and balances were put in place to prevent the search from taking off in the wrong direction. Let's examine some of the balances that keep CEO searches on track and on target:

- *A balanced time frame.* If you start a search prematurely or if you try to rush one through, you're likely to pick the wrong candidate. If Tom had started his search when he originally called me, he would have been handicapped because he lacked a solid, board-certified candidate specification. Companies need to think and talk about the specs and define them precisely before starting the search process. Similarly, companies that impose an absurdly tight deadline often end up making poor choices. Typically, searches require five to seven months. That time is necessary for thorough research; selection of prospective candidates; interviews, evaluations, and reference-checks; and the narrowing down of choices through committee discussion and formal analysis. Although there are instances when speed is essential, they tend to be the exception. Panicky selection committees often have more time than they think. Mr. Rogers said it best. I recall watching the children's show with my daughters and hearing him sing, "Oh isn't it nice to have the time to do things right."

- *Balanced participation of the key five players.* Boards who exclude the incumbent CEO unbalance the process. Similarly, CEOs who exclude the board commit the same unbalancing crime. When eager, naive CEO candidates are deceived or manipulated in some fashion, this too throws the process off kilter. Book-and-bill search consultants have the same effect. Although it's not always necessary for CHROs to be equal partners in selecting CEOs—the CHRO at MassMutual served an important but not coequal role—their input and ideas should be solicited; they may identify problems or potential that others can miss. At MassMutual, the chief human resources officer played an important role in discussing compensation and selecting an outside compensation consultant to work with the committee to move the process forward.

- *Balanced knowledge.* The more a company knows about its internal candidates, its strategy, and the type of leader that is right for the company's future, the better able it is to make a wise selection. Too often, however, this knowledge is unbalanced. Perhaps the CEO is keeping key information about the company to himself. Perhaps the board has failed to keep itself informed about the company's business, competitive challenges, evolving resources, and so on.

• *Balanced perception.* I've seen companies hire people based almost exclusively on their reputation. The media dubs a particular top executive a star, and the rush is on to appoint him CEO of this or that company. Invariably, when General Electric named a new CEO to replace Jack Welch, the search firms descended on the two internal candidates who weren't named to the position. GE has a great reputation, and a number of its senior executives are considered brilliant leaders. This perception needs to be tested and customized to a given company's situation, however. A great leader for Company A might be a horrendous leader for Company B. To achieve balanced perception, there must be democratic participation in the selection process, and everyone must do their homework to determine whether perception is reality for a specific organization.

The Internal Ideal

People go outside for CEOs when they've failed to develop an internal group of succession candidates. Sometimes circumstances change so quickly that there isn't time or opportunity to develop people properly. In most instances, however, internal candidates aren't developed because not much thought is given to the issue. Over the years, I've observed a number of companies that enjoyed a solid group of internal people who were eminently qualified to become CEO. This doesn't mean that they were all chosen for the job, but their organizations at least had an internal candidate as an option. To groom internal people for the CEO position, these organizations

• Had a method in place for evaluating talent and began evaluating it early in people's careers

- Possessed a developmental process that measures the *promotability* of future leaders for responsibilities at different leadership stages
- Enjoyed a management culture that believes in moving people around and measuring their performance in a variety of positions
- Identified whether a particular leader was best suited for growing, maintaining, or turning around a business
- Allowed people opportunities to fail and learn from these failures
- Created a detailed portfolio on individuals by the time they reached the senior executive level, including their strengths, weaknesses, and leadership style
- Kept the board engaged in the aforementioned process

Any organization that does these things will have created a pool of leadership talent from which to draw. Given the candidate profile, a selection committee can know exactly what they have internally and who is suited to the role at a particular time. In the best of circumstances, they will have five or more people who are potential candidates and who have held a succession of jobs over a period of at least ten years. Because they've been observed and measured in a variety of businesses and leadership positions, the selection committee will be able to quickly assess who is best qualified to take over the organization.

But even if organizations have developed their own people so that they have solid CEO candidates, the ideal scenario doesn't always play out. In some instances, companies suffer from a "grass is always greener" syndrome and believe outside candidates are always better than internal ones. What is even more common, some boards are afraid to select an internal candidate because of the potentially negative repercussions. A board member once said to me: "We have two terrific internal candidates, but we're afraid if we select one, we'll lose the other." No question, this is a possibility.

But it's a mistake to disembowel a great internal candidate because of fears of losing a valuable executive. If the candidates are evaluated perceptively and fairly and one is deemed better than the other, much more is gained by choosing the first choice and losing the second choice than going outside and hiring someone who isn't as well-suited to the job as either internal person.

Organizations sometimes fail to recognize that selecting an internal candidate is just as difficult—if not more difficult—than selecting an outside one. Just look at Coca-Cola and Procter & Gamble, two leading organizations that named internal candidates as CEOs only to see them come up short after a relatively brief tenure. Boards need to be responsible for developing and setting guidelines for selecting internal people. This means determining how to prevent the departing CEO from interfering with the new CEO (if the internal CEO was mentored by the outgoing CEO, this is critical) and devising a useful method to measure internal candidates against each other as well as the position.

The Ideal Varies According to the Situation

Sometimes the ideal process isn't possible—or it's more difficult to achieve—because of the circumstances. For instance, when a CEO leaves a company abruptly and unexpectedly, the organization is usually caught flat-footed (especially if they've failed to develop solid internal candidates). Or an organization may be in desperate straits; the board has fired the CEO and is looking for someone who can get the company back on track before it's too late. In another instance, the ideal is difficult to achieve because the CEO who initiated the search is withholding crucial information from the board about the company, and this lack of information causes the board to select the wrong person.

I've seen many selection mistakes made when boards rush forward and insist that a CEO must be found immediately. Typically, a company undergoes a crisis and the board asks the CEO to leave or the CEO resigns on his own. The board becomes nervous, contacts a search consultant, and asks them to identify a replacement within the month. Because the board isn't interested in learning about the search process or even playing a significant role in it, it simply issues a command and expects it be carried out with all due speed.

What should happen in this situation is that the board calls a time-out and elects one of its members to serve as interim CEO. Then, within a week of this appointment, the board starts defining the specs for the position, reaches consensus, and begins the search.

Admittedly, the ideal scenarios described in this book are most likely to take place in companies with psychologically healthy CEOs and knowledgeable, involved boards. The ideal is also facilitated when companies are in great shape, with terrific products and services and wonderful balance sheets. I think it was Warren Buffet who once said that he liked to invest in companies that were momentum-oriented, possessed a great infrastructure, and could be run by a dunce.

Most organizations need far more than a dunce can provide. Though your company may not be in a position to achieve the close-to-ideal scenario of a MassMutual, you'll find that the tips and techniques in the chapters that follow will help you take the steps necessary to make an equally sound selection choice.

Chapter Three

Real-World Issues

The Complexities That Foul Up
the Selection Process

At this point, you may be asking yourself a question that I've asked myself many times: *Why is it so difficult to fix a process that seems so dysfunctional?*

Why can't the five players in the CEO selection dynamic get together and right the wrongs in the process? A pessimist might answer: Because it's not in their best interests to do so. Certainly, some CEOs and board members are shortsighted and want to maintain the status quo, but that's not the right answer. Generally speaking, the individuals in our dynamic are highly intelligent, talented and well-meaning. In a perfect world, they would be glad to work together in ways that would lead to the selection of the right CEO.

Unfortunately, it's not a perfect world. Rather, the world in which CEOs are selected is complex, ambiguous, and paradoxical. Sometimes, it seems as though a board has made a horrendous CEO selection when in fact there are solid reasons for the choice they made. In other instances, it appears initially as though a company made an astute move in naming an internal candidate as the CEO successor because everything went so well during that first year, but with five years of hindsight everyone realizes the company should have found an outside candidate.

Let's look at the underlying complexities and issues that make choosing CEOs such a difficult task.

What a Tangled Web We Weave

Throughout my career, I've read news stories describing brilliant or bungled CEO selections that have been woefully inaccurate. Because I was involved in the searches or knew people who were, I was aware of issues invisible to the reporter's eye. For instance, one story talked about how a company after "thorough and exhaustive analysis" decided to bypass internal candidates and go outside for a CEO successor. The article reported about how the board determined and top management agreed that the organization needed a leader with "broader experience and a fresh perspective." What the article failed to mention was that this organization hadn't developed an effective talent pipeline or succession plan, the board and incumbent CEO had informally selected three internal candidates and tested them by giving them a series of challenging assignments, and that each of the three candidates had demonstrated through these tests that they were woefully unqualified for the CEO position. Because these were the company's best and brightest people, the board had no choice but to look elsewhere for a chief executive. If the article had been written to reflect reality, the reader would understand that the company was guilty of not developing its own leadership talent and went outside because their own cupboard was bare.

The following are the most common obstacles, complications, and situations that prevent organizations from adopting the balanced approach advocated in earlier chapters:

• *Choosing the wrong person on purpose.* Sometimes selection becomes a bit Machiavellian. I've seen boards and incumbent CEOs who determine that the company culture needs to be shaken up, and it needs to be shaken up immediately. Perhaps they're desperate to embark on a new strategy more in line with a changing market, or they want to position the company for sale in a rapidly consolidating industry. Consequently, they are more concerned about getting someone in quickly who can spark change rather than selecting the ideal person for the job. Sometimes boards decide that the "real" successor is in the company but needs a few years of seasoning before he's ready to take over. In these instances, they hire caretaker CEOs who aren't particularly right for the job but won't break anything either.

Sometimes choosing the wrong person for the right reasons makes sense. If a great internal candidate exists, you might need to buy him a few years of seasoning time. If the organization can get by with marginal leadership for a few years, perhaps this strategy is appropriate. Of course, choosing the wrong CEO is also a strategy that can be abused and do serious harm to a company. It can be used by an egocentric CEO who chooses a weak candidate to preserve his own power and longevity or by a board that's too detached or incompetent to put in the time to make the right choice.

• *Believing an individual has earned the top spot.* When Durk Jager was named CEO at P&G and experienced numerous problems during his tenure and was let go, it became clear he was the wrong person for the job. Criticisms against Jager suggested he was too great a change agent for P&G and that his style rankled the rank and file. In other words, he pushed for change too hard and too fast. Given these and other traits that must have been apparent to everyone before he was selected for the top spot, why was he named CEO? I asked this question of a P&G board member, and he told me, "Because a majority of the board felt he had earned it."

In one sense, this notion of *earning it* is an admirable tradition. If someone pays his dues, works hard, and does everything that's asked of him, rewarding him with what he wants seems the honorable thing to do. Unfortunately, it's not always what's best for the organization. Most companies have come to realize that rewarding seniority or top performance with a promotion can backfire. In the former instance (and especially in this day and age), you may be rewarding someone simply because he was unable to get a job somewhere else. In the latter case, you're assuming that if someone can produce results in one position, he can produce equal or better results in another; the reality is that the new position may require different skills and values that weren't required by the former job.

Earning it, therefore, often is a criterion that obviates all the other, more important criteria. The CEO position should not be a reward for a job well done but because individual experience, track record of performance, and expertise match up with the organization's current and future strategic requirements.

- *Neglecting succession planning.* Sometimes organizations want to follow an intelligent CEO selection protocol but can't because they don't know who their top internal people are or they've failed to develop them. It's astonishing that board members don't know who their five or six top contenders for the CEO position are, or that they lack a program to rotate these contenders through different assignments and observe and measure the results relative to CEO job requirements. As a result, the selection process becomes unbalanced because of an internal flaw. The incumbent CEO may suddenly decide to retire (or leave the company for any number of reasons) and the board is caught short; they assumed the CEO would be there for at least another five years. They may end up choosing the wrong internal candidate because of their lack of knowledge, or they may decide to ignore inside people because they haven't developed and assessed them properly. In either case, the chances of finding a top-performing CEO are lessened.

- *Hiring the wrong person for the right reasons.* A number of years back, an electronics industry company hired me to find a president for a subsidiary. Their president was taking early retirement, but the company seemed to be in great shape. After doing a great deal of interviewing and research, I helped them develop candidate specifications. From all the input I received, I learned that the company's biggest challenge was making the transition to a flatter, more decentralized structure. The current president had embarked on a restructuring as part of a larger corporate effort. I created specs around the need to find someone who had helped another company make a similar transition and was skilled at operating in a team-based environment. Ultimately, we hired an executive who had very impressive credentials related to the spec. Even though he was not particularly strong in some other key areas, his undeniable expertise in helping another electronics company restructure made him an excellent selection—or so it seemed at the time. Following up six months later, I found that the client was very happy with his performance.

A year later, however, I received a call from this company telling me that they were terminating their president, admitting they had made a mistake. It turned out that the previous president had downplayed challenges from foreign competitors in his discussions with the board, in part because he had successfully ignored this threat in the past and assumed he could continue to ignore it. In fact, low-cost foreign competitors were seriously eroding the company's revenues, and one of their new president's shortcomings was a lack of international experience. This company needed a CEO who had a global marketing background rather than one who was adept at team restructuring. At the time of the search, however, none of us could have known that this is what the company needed. We were relying on the exiting CEO's misleading information in our selection thinking.

• *Talking, but not talking straight.* This heading covers a multitude of sins. It may be that the search consultant isn't telling the client that their search parameters are unrealistic. It may be that a board is unwilling to be honest with a CEO who asks them whether they think it would be a problem if he "oversees" the new CEO for the first year; or, as in our previous example, the CEO is deceiving the organization; or the human resources chief is unwilling to stand up to the CEO. It doesn't take much to unbalance the process.

After I recruited a CEO successor for a Fortune 100 company with a mandate for change, the retiring CEO approached his board of directors because he felt his successor—who had by then only been in office for six months—was, in his words, "killing the company." This retiring CEO wasn't talking straight with the board; he was letting his ego and his difficulty in letting go of the CEO position shape his words. Because this chief executive had contributed a great deal to the organization over the years and had strong relationships with a number of board members, the board could easily have given in and not talked straight to the former CEO. They could have given him "oversight" power or even fired the new CEO. Fortunately, they did neither but told the retired CEO straight up that they thought his successor was doing a good job relative to the future strategy for the company. He left an angry man and subsequently sold all his stock in a fit of pique. His successor went on to lead the company to great success.

• *Hiring the wrong person with the right qualifications.* When Bob Allen hired John Walter as COO and potential CEO successor at AT&T, he was hiring someone who seemed eminently qualified for the CEO position. As a powerful CEO, Allen used his influence to make sure his candidate was hired. Because he basically ran the search himself (his chief HR officer assisted him), Allen bypassed a number of outside CEO succession candidates who probably would have been better choices but would have been unwilling to assume a COO position on the promise of being named CEO at some point in the future. Although credentials are important, they shouldn't be the only or even the primary criteria.

When powerful CEOs assume they know best and exclude board members from succession discussions and decisions, they unbalance the process. They may have good intentions and truly believe that they have a special insight into who is the right candidate, but their judgment may be clouded by their ego and desire to preserve their legacy, and an overly accommodating HR chief or search consultant can compound the mistake.

• *Maintaining a culture of entitlement.* Strong cultures are terrific, and I admire mission-focused organizations in which people take great pride in their accomplishments. Sometimes, however, this pride becomes hubris and leads to a fall. When CEOs and board members, especially, feel that *we're one special company* to the point of infallibility, there can be problems in succession planning and selection. Typically, these organizations are wary of outsiders. For this reason, they're extremely reluctant to look outside for a CEO, even if their circumstances cry out for a fresh leadership perspective.

Many times, cultures of entitlement are found in aging "legacy" companies where board members serve long terms, CEOs remain on the job for years, and former CEOs are installed on the board and given offices. In these cultures, no one wants to change anything, especially the process by which CEOs are hired. Organizational inbreeding is the consequence. Once upon a time, the leadership qualities of the CEO were appropriate, but over the years these qualities remain static while the environment changes. No one who participates in the CEO selection process is willing or able to admit that the company's esteemed culture and strategies need to be changed and someone has to be hired who can change them.

• *Succumbing to the natural pull of personal bias.* Perhaps it's only human nature, but board members often succumb to their own prejudices about who should be running their organizations. Many board members are current and former CEOs, and consciously or not, they look at the CEO position and think, What would I do if I were in charge? Then they search for the candidate who would carry out their wishes. Their biases pull the real specs off center. These board members honestly believe they're being objective, but because they have CEO experience, their background makes it difficult to be objective. They know what worked for them, and it's sometimes difficult for them to see why it might not work for the company in question.

• *Remaining in the shadow cast by the outgoing CEO.* When the incumbent CEO has done great things for a company and has been in office for a long time, boards are tempted to hire clones. The incumbent CEO won't admit the company needs someone with different ideas and experience, and the board can't imagine insulting their highly accomplished chief executive officer in this manner. Boards want to please outgoing CEOs who have done terrific jobs, and they often believe the way to please them is by hiring their protégés or outsiders who have received the CEO's blessing.

Again, this belief skews the process. Instead of objectively assessing whether a clone should be hired, there is unquestioning acceptance that such a hire makes sense. In reality, the shadow cast by even the most powerful and successful CEOs fades rather quickly. When these CEOs leave—and I mean when they really leave both their jobs and the physical premises of their companies—their influence quickly wanes. I've seen board members regret trying to please an incumbent CEO. When that CEO is long gone, those board members are left trying to clean up the mess of a bad choice. More often than not, this bad choice is an insider.

Simplifying the Complexities

To a certain extent, organizations are at the mercy of their environments. There's not always much they can do about unconscious biases of board members, the deceptions of a former CEO, or a decision to select a less-than-ideal candidate to buy time for an ideal (but unseasoned) candidate. Though some complicating factors are unavoidable, others can be eliminated or minimized by certain actions. Here are some actions that will help you keep the complexities at bay and the selection process balanced:

• *Make ten years the organization's norm for CEO tenure.* The shadow cast by the outgoing CEO won't be as long (or as long-lasting) if he hasn't been in office for more than ten years. When people hold down the CEO position for fifteen, twenty, or more years, they become almost deified within the organization, and it's very difficult for board members, the incoming CEO, or anyone else to defy their wishes. Many times, this mythic CEO doesn't even have to say anything; people anticipate his preferences and respond accordingly. Unlike years ago, today's rapid changes demand periodic shifts in leadership. This time frame also aids succession planning. Bill George, the CEO of Medtronic, Inc., was an outside candidate who told the board that he intended to step down after ten years as CEO *during the discussion phase* when I was recruiting him to be CEO of Medtronic.

• *Address executive pipeline and succession issues at least once a year.* Companies that don't know whether they have viable internal CEO candidates or have failed to develop that talent have only themselves to blame when a CEO selection goes bad. Similarly, boards must ask *What if our CEO gets run over by a truck tomorrow?* and plan for various succession scenarios. This needs to be done on a regular basis. The board, the incumbent CEO, and the HR chief must make a commitment to identify and develop three to five potential successors. Companies that do so annually not only are likely to have a good successor ready to take over but also increase their executive bench strength. It may also make sense to hire an executive search consultant to conduct a benchmark search, comparing internal with external talent.

• *Watch for foreboding signs of eroding leadership.* Things get complicated when problems have spiraled out of control. When organizations have been losing executive talent for years, it's difficult to conduct a CEO search in a balanced manner (since there are no viable internal candidates to consider). When companies are losing business and talent to the competition, the search for a CEO often is tinged with desperation, and the search committee focuses on finding a star to save them. By watching for these signs and doing something about them quickly, it's less likely that complicating factors will hamper a search.

• *Assess CEO openness and honesty.* If a CEO doesn't share mistakes, problems, challenges, and other bad news with the board, it's likely that they will be conducting their next CEO search with a false set of specifications. As we've seen, CEOs who hide bad news or mislead their boards create situations where the wrong CEO is hired for the right reasons. If the board had access to all the relevant information, they probably wouldn't hire that particular person. Therefore, boards must hold CEOs accountable and ask them the type of probing questions that elicit truthful answers. Confronting chief executives about problems or inconsistencies is part of the board's governance responsibilities and will make their job of selecting a new CEO that much simpler.

• *Determine whether the HR chief is a henchman for the CEO.* In organizations where the HR head simply does the CEO's bidding, it's often a sign that a poor job is being done in building an executive pipeline and in CEO succession planning. HR chiefs who don't sit as an equal at the management table take orders, or won't take the initiative to lay the groundwork for choosing the next leader of the company; they serve the CEO rather than the organization or shareholders. When HR executives are essentially removed from the five-person dynamic, complications set in. When no one is assessing internal talent or providing a search consultant with objective insights and information, it becomes much more difficult to conduct a search. Neither the CEO nor the board should toler-ate an HR chief who lacks the business acumen and willingness to use it to identify viable internal and external CEO candidates. Purely administrative or bureaucratic HR chiefs unbalance the five-person dynamic, and this causes problems when their insights and expertise are required.

CEOs might consider having their line executives do a stint in the HR department as a partial solution. Too often, other execu-tives view the HR chief as nothing more than an administrative functionary because they lack any familiarity with HR. It may be that the HR head isn't a henchman for the CEO, but everyone assumes he is out of ignorance. Requiring other executives to rub shoulders with HR people will help them develop an appreciation for what they actually do and make them less likely to jump to con-clusions about the HR chief's role.

- *Beware of incestuous relationships between boards and retiring CEOs.* It becomes very difficult for boards to say no to CEOs who they consider pals. Many times, board members and the CEO main-tain vacation homes in the same community, belong to the same clubs, and attend external functions together. Although a strong relationship between a CEO and his board members is natural, this intimacy complicates CEO selection in all sorts of ways. For one thing, board members are reluctant to go against the CEO's wishes for a successor. For another, boards are perfectly willing to supply their retired friend with an office and grant him a position on the board for an indefinite term. This often makes the new CEO (who lacks this relationship with board members) uncomfortable and can limit his authority. Though it's sometimes difficult for boards to avoid these compromising situations, one thing they can do is set clear ground rules about what the retired CEO's role is and how long he'll serve in this role. When these ground rules don't exist—when the retired CEO is not required to leave after a year or is permitted to interfere with the new CEO's decisions—the operating environment becomes a mess. When Jim Hardymon retired as chairman and CEO of Textron, Inc., he broke a historic trend for the retired Textron CEO to remain on the board until age seventy. He left the board and made himself available to his successor Lewis Campbell on an as-needed advisory basis.

• *Strive for board and executive diversity.* The complicating factors of personal bias and a lack of straight talk are likely to creep into the process in homogeneous environments. Exclusion (de facto or otherwise) of minorities, women, and relatively young turks creates a devastating sameness of opinion. Similarly, when all board members have long-term relationships and have the same backgrounds (especially when they're from the same generation), they lack the diversity of experience that leads to innovative ideas about who should run the company. When everyone has the same personal bias, it tends to shape the selection process and precludes open-ended discussions. In addition, when all the internal executive talents are cut from the same cloth, there's less likelihood that one of them will emerge as a viable candidate. A lack of diversity means a lack of opinions and options, and this makes it difficult for any company to engage in the spirited discussions and creative thinking essential to the CEO identification, development, and selection process.

One Final, Ironic Factor

I would be remiss if I ignored one other factor that can confuse the issue of CEO selection. Some board members involved in the selection process profess to be too busy or don't take their stewardship seriously (including some board succession committee heads).

Either they don't want to interfere with the CEO, or they believe that selecting a CEO isn't that significant a task to warrant much of their time, or they feel that even if they make a bad selection, it won't do much harm. In either case, they don't invest much energy or effort in making a wise selection. Ironically, this simplistic approach complicates matters.

The other issue is the invisible negative repercussions of a poorly chosen CEO. There are cases of CEOs who were incompetent, myopic, and even fraudulent but whose organizations didn't seem to suffer great harm during their tenure. Even if revenues declined when they were in charge, a new CEO came on board and revenues rebounded. Therefore, it seems as though a poor selection doesn't have a serious impact.

In fact, poor selection always has a serious impact, but it's not always apparent to the naked eye. Sometimes, of course, there are devastating financial and market-losing consequences. Other times, however, the ramifications may be losing good talent and hiring mediocre talent. Or the negative results might not show up for a while—an acquisition that ultimately costs the company money and people.

Perhaps the most serious repercussion—and the one that's most difficult to measure—is a loss of momentum. Poorly chosen CEOs can cause an energetic, forward-moving company to lose its momentum gradually and almost imperceptibly. Their words and ideas don't rally the troops. They bring in a management team that lacks sufficient creativity and knowledge; B people hire C people. They make a series of small, seemingly insignificant errors. A few good people leave. Market share drops a bit. Eventually, everything conspires to slow the company's growth and diminish the morale and productivity of its people. In some cases, the company is acquired.

Unless CEO-selectors recognize this fact, they may not devote significant amounts of time, energy, and ingenuity to a task that demands all these things.

Chapter Four

The Psychologically Healthy CEO

Jack Neff, CEO, Largesse Corporation:

I really enjoy the power that comes with being CEO of Largesse Corporation. To be specific, I relish not just the perks of the position but the lifestyle. From being around fellow CEOs at the Business Roundtable to entertaining customers at Old Elm and Loblolly, it's a terrific job. In fact, we just took delivery of a new Citation, and my wife and I are looking forward to our next trip to Europe to visit distributors (not to mention playing golf in Scotland after we finish the working part of the trip). As a CEO, people know who I am, and I can feel their attention and respect when I walk into a room. I'm on two prestigious NYSE corporate boards, and I've been proposed for membership at Pine Valley. Life is good.

What isn't so good is dealing with a declining stock price and running an old-economy company in a new-economy world. Once again, some of our competitors have been cutting prices and eroding our share of the market through overt and covert messages about how we're the high-cost producers. We're also the highest-quality producers, a fact they neglect to add. Even more troubling, a large vulture investor has acquired a major ownership stake in Largesse, and I'm told that their fund manager plans to come out next week and meet me. No doubt, he will be accompanied by some young punk M.B.A. who will insist on telling me about my company and lecture me about six sigma, e-commerce, and the like and be shocked to learn that I don't have a computer on my credenza. I have consultants' reports in my desk drawer bringing me new ideas, but what's wrong with the proven way we run this company? For decades we've been a market leader, and it really riles me when someone else tells me how to do my job. I've heard the whispers: "Jack doesn't 'get' e-commerce; Jack never had any international experience; Jack is a traditionalist." But you know what? We have a rich tradition, and it's sustained this company over the years through many so-called radical changes in our industry and society.

I admit this is a great setup for me and my wife; she loves the CEO lifestyle too. Socially, her best friend is Sam's wife, and Sam's been a buddy of mine for years. I like having Sam on the board. Not only has he been a great director since he joined us fifteen years ago, but he's also diffused a number of potential challenges to my leadership at board meetings. Once, one of the other directors insisted that strategy discussions should take place at every board meeting and that my operating guys should make presentations to them. In addition, he suggested that board members visit business units on their own (though he allowed that they should notify me first). What nonsense! As was the suggestion by the chairman of our compensation committee that our HR chief prepare a list of internal candidates as part of a CEO succession plan. He felt that the board should review these candidates even though I'm at least two years away from retirement. Noses in, fingers out, has always been my philosophy about how a good board functions, and my directors know this.

In any case, Jerry Martin is my choice to succeed me. Besides, after I retire in two or three years, I intend to stay on for five years as nonexecutive chairman, so I'll still be in control. Nonetheless, I'm glad that Sam has agreed to chair a new CEO succession committee. I can count on him to control the process and keep other board members in line. I can deal with Jerry, who I know is impatient to take over, but he's going to have to pay his dues, just as I did years ago before our previous CEO took his sweet time in leaving. I've made it clear to everyone that the CEO's job is Jerry's to lose, and if anyone doesn't like that decision, they are under no obligation to continue to serve on Largesse's board.

As you may have gathered, Jack is not a psychologically healthy CEO. He is, however, a powerful CEO who will control his board of directors and twist the CEO succession process to meet his own needs. We'll meet other key players associated with the fictional Largesse Corporation in the following chapters. Here, though, I've shared the innermost thoughts of the company's CEO to help you glimpse how a psychologically unhealthy chief executive can damage the process. While Jack is a composite, he is only slightly exaggerated from some real CEOs I've met over the years. While they may have developed an outer persona that disguises these thoughts and allows them to present themselves as highly professional, competent, and even charismatic, the hubris that drives them is just beneath the surface.

Not all CEOs are like this. Many psychologically healthy alternative models exist. What I hope to do here is present one of these models and demonstrate how CEOs can contribute enormously to the choice of an appropriate successor and keep the selection process in balance.

A Fine Line

Realistically, most CEOs are neither raving egotists nor self-actualized human beings. Instead, they occupy a middle ground where the line between psychologically healthy and unhealthy is easily crossed. Any CEO who has reached this capstone position invariably has a strong ego and is proud and ambitious. It's only when that pride becomes hubris and the oblivious narcissist becomes blind that the CEO selection process is corrupted.

Bill George, chairman of Medtronic, Inc., provides another way of making this differentiation. He refers to any healthy executive as someone who is "comfortable in his skin." In other words, he's comfortable with what he's accomplished as CEO and the legacy that he's leaving; he's come to terms with his impending retirement and doesn't feel compelled to prove something to his successor, the board, or the industry. A CEO who is uncomfortable in his skin, however, believes he must continue to do (or not do) things in order to preserve his legacy; he fears the unknown abyss of retirement and the loss of recognition as he transitions from *who's who* to *who's he*. His self-esteem could actually be shaky.

The unhealthy CEO agonizes about how his friends, neighbors, and loved ones will perceive him once he's an ordinary citizen. This CEO may have asked the board to push back the mandatory retirement age for him; he may also have insisted that the company provide him with an office, a corporate jet, and a seat on the board for a number of years after he's retired. This type of person has no retirement plans that he's eagerly anticipating and often lacks a clear idea of what he'll do once he stops working. Pity the successor who is selected to follow this individual.

The healthy CEO certainly may have some anxiety about life after work—it's only natural for any person to worry about this radical transition—but it's not a paralyzing fear. On a good day, he views retirement as a twenty-year opportunity for replenishment and has a number of things he wants to accomplish during this time. Although he's willing to help his successor make the transition, he is unwilling to hang around indefinitely; he is eager to get on with the next stage of his life. Typically, this person has planned a full schedule for himself in retirement, including visiting grandkids, taking vacations, doing consulting, sitting on boards, and giving back via the not-for-profit sector.

When you look at someone like Jack Welch or even a football coach like the late Vince Lombardi, you may think that they're demonstrably psychologically unhealthy. After all, isn't it unhealthy to be incredibly demanding and maniacally dedicated to their work? I don't think so. What keeps people like Welch and Lombardi on the healthy side of the line is their sense of perspective; they are healthy narcissists. As dedicated and demanding as they are, they also recognize their flaws and humanity. As talented as they are, they also understand that there are others of equal talent out there. Though they receive a tremendous amount of adulation that might turn lesser men's heads, they remain grounded. A quote attributed to Alexander the Great captures this quality best. Alexander, who was the conqueror of most of the then-known world, received more praise than any CEO (well, any CEO perhaps except Welch). For this reason, he hired someone to walk beside him and whisper in his ear, "Thou art only a man." Today's healthy CEO has colleagues, confidants, and often a spouse who remind him of this fact (or he reminds himself).

Finally, people fall to either side of the line based on their feelings about productivity. One newly retired CEO said to me: "I woke up in the morning, and I had the compulsion to be productive." CEOs are always doing things. Their schedules are filled with myriad activities, and even when they're home or on vacation, they're working on business-related matters via phone, e-mail, and faxes. To cut off this frenetic activity is traumatic for even healthy CEOs; there's a huge void in their lives. A psychologically unhealthy CEO, for instance, has nothing outside of his work. He lacks hobbies and may even prioritize work over family. He lacks empathy. Although this is an extreme case, it represents a type whose dread of retirement is well-founded; this person may become an alcoholic or depressed when he no longer is engaged in his work routine. Fearing this lack of productivity, the unhealthy CEO manipulates the succession process to ensure that he'll be around as long as possible and have a lot to do even if a new CEO is chosen. Healthy CEOs, however, learn to channel their energy into other endeavors. I know retired CEOs who dedicate themselves to their golf games, start small entrepreneurial businesses, sit on several boards, and use their talents on behalf of charitable organizations. Few CEOs are well-suited to sitting around the house doing nothing, and those that find an outlet for their energy before retiring will do a much better job in choosing a successor.

Signs That a CEO Is Unbalancing the Process

Too often, boards don't realize the harm unhealthy CEOs are doing to the selection process. In some instances, the CEOs themselves have a strong sense of entitlement and are unaware that they're doing any damage; they've rationalized their actions and simply don't understand that they're making choices based on fear and ego rather than objectivity. Let's look at some of the most common signs that a CEO is causing the process to go awry:

- *Chooses a mirror-image successor.* Typically, this choice is an internal candidate the CEO has been grooming for his job. The successor's leadership style, business philosophy, and even his personality are similar to his mentor. Although in certain instances it may make sense to find a CEO candidate who leads much as his predecessor did, many times it's a mistake. In a rapidly changing world, organizations need new leaders who can evolve their strategies and cultures, not replicate them. The unhealthy CEO deludes himself into believing that if he finds someone just like himself, this new CEO will help the company enjoy the same success that he helped it achieve. In reality, such a choice often dooms a company to mediocrity or even obsolescence. Though this statement may be a psychological reach, some CEOs seem to desire a form of immortality, and by choosing a successor who mirrors them, they at least extend their work life by ten or fifteen years.

- *Chooses a below-average candidate.* In a sense, this a variation on the previous point. As much as the CEO wants to replace himself with a mirror image candidate, he determines that no such animal exists and decides (unconsciously) to sabotage the process. The most common form of sabotage is for the CEO to select a candidate who he knows isn't up to the job. Such as choice accomplishes a number of dysfunctional goals. For one thing, it will cause everyone to recognize what a great job he did when he was CEO and tell him, "Gee, John, things haven't been the same since you left." For another, it causes the board to ask the retired CEO to stick around because the new CEO lacks the experience or expertise to go it alone (or he makes mistakes and the board asks the old CEO to lend a hand). Again, this sabotage isn't usually conscious. The outgoing chief executive can justify his choice to himself in all sorts of ways: Mark will grow into the job, he's young and willing to learn, or Jill might lack international experience, but she's good at building teams that compensate for areas where she's weak.

• *Creates an uncertain environment.* Some CEOs embark on restructuring or repositioning strategies near the end of their tenure, throwing the company into turmoil and providing their successors with huge challenges. In some instances, these CEOs are trying to create situations in which they're needed. They want the board to tell them: Stay past your retirement date and help us deal with the program you started. When this CEO can't postpone his retirement any longer, the successor is often left with a mess that evolves from months or years of an uncertain strategy.

• *Fails to build a pipeline of potential candidates.* When a CEO leaves the talent cupboard bare, it's a bad sign. The problem isn't just that the company is forced to go outside for candidates. A CEO may have avoided the task of grooming a successor until it's too late, and when he realizes that he's neglected this crucial function (often because he was unable to face the reality that his reign had to end at some point), he sometimes hastily identifies internal candidates who aren't qualified to be CEO. Unfortunately, their lack of qualifications aren't always apparent to board members operating from a distance. Failing to develop successors is embarrassing, and some CEOs, rather than admit this failing, resort to extraordinary measures. In one instance, a CEO actually helped arrange a merger for his company before retiring, handing off the succession issue to the CEO and board of the other company. The important question is: Has a CEO invested time and energy developing a pool of qualified candidates over the years? If he hasn't—or if he just started one year before he will retire—you can anticipate trouble.

• *Looks for superman.* Some CEOs make a great show of looking for a successor but it's just that: all show and no substance. I know of the chairman and CEO of a large corporation who has been shopping for a CEO for almost three years. He's now on his third search consulting firm, and though each firm has presented him with a number of candidates, none have been good enough for him. Although it's fine to be selective, there comes a point where selectivity devolves into nitpicking. Beware of the CEO who is willing to comb the world for the perfect CEO. As we'll see a bit later, recognizing that this perfect creature is mythical is an attribute of a psychologically healthy CEO. There is no such thing as a perfect candidate.

• *Starts a "horse race."* Perhaps of all the signs, this is the one that is most insidious. If horse races have not become ubiquitous in CEO succession circles, they certainly have become more common than ever before, as the following true story indicates.

A CEO of a large manufacturing company declared that he would be retiring within the year, and he announced that three internal candidates would be considered for his spot, and a decision would be made six months hence. During the next six months, these three candidates were on pins and needles. Not one of them was willing to talk straight to the CEO; they were so conscious that a wrong word might put them out of the running that they looked at each interaction with the CEO as a chance to score points. They also played politics to the hilt, calling in favors and forming coalitions that they thought might influence the board and the CEO to select them over the others.

When one of the candidates was selected, the two others left the organization within the year, furious that they weren't chosen and angry with the one who was picked. Not only did the company lose two very talented executives, but the one who was named CEO was not particularly well-qualified to lead the company and was asked to leave by the board after two years.

Horse races focus on the short term. Typically, boards or incumbent CEOs judge candidates based on performance over a very short stretch, where all sorts of factors can skew the results. Horse races are often won by the best presenters; the person who gets up and makes an eloquent speech to the board wins the race. This is as opposed to a long-term "race" in which candidates' potentials for promotion are observed in a variety of key situations over a period of years, and their performance is measured against well-conceived CEO specs, such as in General Electric's development culture.

Publicizing horse races, too, creates all sorts of problems. Making the race public focuses so much attention—both internally and externally—on the candidates that it's impossible for anyone to perform normally. Divisiveness is the end product of these intense sprints to the finish, and they create lowered morale and a potentially dangerous exodus of talent.

Highly egocentric CEOs love horse races. They get a thrill out of choosing contestants and watching them compete against each other. In some cases, CEOs who aren't egocentric elect to create these races believing that the right candidate will somehow emerge victorious. In reality, all that happens is that one person puts on a better show than the others, and the horse race simply covers up the fact that succession planning and development were neglected in previous years.

Putting the Company and the Shareholders First

When an incumbent CEO chooses the right successor, he invariably considers this an important part of his job and gets an early start on it. When I recruited Bill George as CEO of medical device-maker Medtronic, Inc., he told the board during interviews that he intended to serve as CEO for no more than ten years. Almost from the beginning, he was on the lookout for successor candidates. Because Medtronic was an $800 million company when Bill joined them and was expanding rapidly, the board wanted the new CEO to develop people to run the $3 billion company it was becoming. When it came to succession, just about everyone on their existing management team lacked the experience to head a $3 billion company, so Bill together with his board and chief HR officer began recruiting the right type of talent to the company and creating a development culture. One of these people was Art Collins, whom I recruited as executive vice president–international. Art joined the company from Abbott Laboratories, where his successful track record as head of their diagnostics group was well-known and documented. He was recruited with the understanding that he would be the CEO successor, with the proviso that he demonstrate success in international endeavors as well as COO. He would take over for Bill when he retired, even though Bill made it clear he wasn't leaving for several years. During this time, Bill gave Art a variety of assignments, all of which he handled expertly and demonstrated to the company and the board that he was the right person for the job. If Art had fallen short on these assignments, the company could have looked at other candidates. But because he handled them so well, everyone agreed he was the right choice for the job.

In Art, Bill found someone who was a good match for the company. A truly healthy CEO looks for a good match between a candidate's skills and experiences and the organization's strategic needs. Art was the right executive for Medtronic at the time, and Bill saw the succession possibility from the start and tested it over the years, also sharing his feelings and observations with the board. In April 2001, Art was elected CEO of Medtronic, which is now a diverse, global $5 billion company.

This is all easier said than done. Many times I'll ask CEOs the following question as they're weighing the choices of potential successors: Are you standing in your shoes or your shareholders' shoes?

More often than not, the answer is their own shoes. Even the most psychologically healthy of chief executives might answer this way. The difference is that either through someone else's prompting or on their own, they recognize this fact. They realize that they want a given individual to succeed them because they've mentored him and have a lot invested in the person's career. Sometimes they come to understand that their choice has to with preserving the company's tradition rather than building its future. Awareness of whether they're making a choice for personal reasons or for ones that will benefit the company is crucial. The psychologically healthy CEO is willing to choose a successor who might not agree with him or continue his strategies but who will give the company its best chance of doing well strategically in the coming years.

When CEOs put their heads on the pillow at night and contemplate their organizations, they often think to themselves: No
one cares about the company as much as I do; no one has as much
knowledge about the company or is better able to lead it. This can
be a healthy thought, but as the CEO approaches the end of his
tenure, it can turn into: No one I choose for my job will be as good
as I was or can do the job without my assistance. Again, the key is
awareness. Leaders need to be aware of their pride and acknowledge
that there is someone out there who will be as good as or better for
the company in the future than they could be. The best CEO-
selectors don't view their departures as an ending but an opportunity for renewal.

Four Necessary Actions of CEOs
in Choosing a Successor

Succession planning should begin the moment a new CEO is
appointed. For many CEOs, searching for a successor is the last
thing on their minds when they're first named to the position. It
should be a responsibility throughout their tenure, and here are four
ways they can carry out this responsibility:

1. *Create a departure timetable.* As a general rule, CEOs
(together with a board succession committee) should start planning
their departure from the company no later than three years before
they're ready to leave. CEOs experience tremendous anxiety when
they realize the end is drawing near, and they start worrying about
what they're going to do after they retire and who is worthy of car-
rying on their legacy. This anxiety affects their objectivity. Leaving
a company—especially a company that has become a significant
part of one's life—is difficult and requires planning if the transition
is to go smoothly. CEOs need to identify a date when they'll retire,
how long they'll be around to help the new CEO, and when they'll
make a clean break from the organization. I'm no fan of a mandatory retirement age, but I'm even less a fan of indeterminate terms

in office. CEOs that keep promising to retire but never quite pull the trigger drive talent out of the organization and make it increasingly difficult to recruit an outside successor.

2. *Hire, develop, and measure a team of potential candidates.* This doesn't just mean hiring a few senior-level executives, it also means getting the best and the brightest young people. Then the key is installing a development process and management culture that ensures they receive a wide range of experience and are measured against performance criteria for a period of years. CEOs and board members should make it their business to interact with these talented executives at least a few times a year to gain firsthand experience of their abilities. The potential candidates should be rotated through a diverse group of domestic and international assignments, and challenged to run a sick business as well as a highly competitive growth business. Observe them without making short-term judgments that can prematurely doom a promising candidate, but keep a record of their performance over the years to make long-term decisions.

3. *Involve direct reports in CEO-like activities over a period of time.* Judging whether internal people have what it takes to be a CEO is a difficult proposition. Too often the incumbent CEO hasn't observed these people in the right types of situations to make an accurate judgment. Part of the problem is that CEOs reserve certain types of activities for themselves and feel it's inappropriate for direct reports to handle them. It's difficult to believe, but many CEOs don't allow their top executives to present to the board of directors or financial analysts. These are prime opportunities for CEOs to see how their executives perform on the firing line in leadership situations and to receive feedback from others about that performance. In addition, CEOs should encourage potential successors to serve as industry leaders or on another company's board of directors. This will help them appreciate the broader, strategic issues that CEOs face.

4. *Involve the board in the process all along the way.* CEOs must give boards a certain measure of independence for the succession

process to be balanced. This means insisting that they talk about CEO succession without the CEO being in the room; it also means exposing the board to different rising executives over the years, insisting that these executives make periodic presentations on a strategic area of the business so the board gets to know them. Just as important, the CEO and his board must discuss and agree about the best role for the CEO during the transition period. How can the company best take advantage of his expertise during the year after he retires? Should he be named nonexecutive chairman for a twelve-month interim period to ease the transition? Should the board find him an off-premise office and give him a consulting contract to advise the board? Or is it best for everyone concerned if the outgoing CEO makes a clean break from the company? Different companies are going to answer these questions in different ways, but it's important to start the dialogue.

Relating to the Other Four Players in the Dynamic

Jack, the CEO of Largesse Corporation, had abysmal relationships with the other people involved in the CEO selection dynamic. From my earlier description, you witnessed how he controlled board members and expected his internal successor and HR chief to do his bidding. Unlike Jack, the psychologically healthy CEO talks straight and establishes open and honest relationships with the four other individuals or groups involved in the selection process. Let's define what each of these relationships should entail:

Human Resources Chief

More than the other four players, HR heads often are left out of the CEO selection loop or viewed as mere bureaucratic functionaries. To a great extent, this is because they gravitate toward staffing work and don't seem interested in or able to perform general management duties. Although they are sometimes derided as being soft and only interested in people issues, their contribution to CEO selection can be significant if CEOs integrate them into top management circles. This means making them part of operating and strategy committees and encouraging them to contribute their ideas. The CEO must make it clear that one of their primary responsibilities is acquiring, developing, and promoting executive talent, including helping the CEO and the board identify the next CEO. Not only must the CEO communicate this responsibility, but he also needs to establish measurements around it. The HR chief should recognize that he's going to be held accountable by the board for maintaining the company's executive talent pipeline. Just as important, the CEO should insist that the HR chief talk straight about the company's talent, even to the point of disagreeing with the CEO about his choices of CEO candidates. When HR chiefs are viewed as the CEO's henchman, they are not taken seriously by boards or other members of top management, and no one believes they can contribute to the selection of a new CEO. This henchman mentality makes HR chiefs reluctant to voice their opinions as well; they're convinced that their role is to carry out the CEO's orders rather than contribute their own ideas about who would make a good candidate. For these reasons, the CEO must make it his business to integrate the HR chief into the process.

Executive Search Consultant

Perhaps the healthiest perspective for a CEO is to view search consultants as providers of a range of services (rather than the singular "fetch" service). Search consultants are the primary advisor to the board search committee. They should help develop the specs for the job, conduct environmental organization studies prior to beginning a search, provide regular progress reports on the search process, develop and interview a large list of prospective candidates (including internal people), winnow the list down to five or six, help the client make the decision (though the CEO should never ask the search consultant, Who should I hire?), advise during compensation negotiations, and contribute to the integration of the selected candidate into the organization. In addition, after the selected candidate has been on the job for six months, the search consultant should follow up to see how the candidate is performing. In many instances, the search consultant gets to know the chosen candidate better than the other members of the selection team (especially if he's an outside candidate). The search consultant also knows the candidate differently. Because the search consultant is the only one who is not a member of the organization, and because he routinely interviews many different CEO candidates for other organizations, he will have insights about the new CEO that others lack. As a result, he can be instrumental in facilitating a transition by advising the incumbent CEO and the board on what things might need to change in order to accommodate the successor's leadership style and transition into a new culture.

Boards

This is obviously a complicated relationship in which personal and professional relationships are mixed. It's also complex because the CEO is dealing with a group of powerful, opinionated business leaders who are beholden to the CEO for their spots on the board. I'll explore these complexities—and how to unravel them—in much more detail in the next chapter. For now, here are the best things a CEO can do to maintain a productive relationships with board members on the CEO succession committee:

- Create the succession committee by picking one member each from the board's compensation, strategy, and governance committees
- Work closely with the committee and HR chief early on in examining internal talent for potential candidates and talk regularly about these candidates at board meetings
- Designate a board member that the CEO can talk honestly with about his wants and needs as retirement approaches, especially as they pertain to his role after he retires

- Establish a contingency plan to replace the CEO if he gets hit by a truck (or some other disaster befalls him)
- Establish a timetable with the board about when they will start talking about CEO succession
- Include the performance of the company's executive talent pipeline as a regular item on the board agenda
- Demand straight talk from the board about succession issues, insisting that they put the company's well-being above friendship with the CEO
- Designate an outside director who will mentor the selected CEO successor

CEO Candidate

Let's deal with internal candidates first. When internal executives know they're being considered for the CEO spot—especially when this knowledge exists years before the CEO retires—they should not feel that this designation prevents them from taking risks, making unpopular decisions, and talking straight with the CEO. In fact, the incumbent CEO should emphasize that these behaviors are desirable. If they perceive that the CEO is keeping a little black book of all their indiscretions, they won't perform well. Just as important, the board won't receive an objective picture of the qualifications for the job, since they'll be holding their tongue when they want to speak and will be indecisive when they should be decisive. Internal candidates must be made aware that their performance is being observed by the board and not just the CEO. Hence, the CEO should make sure that the candidates know that he and the board invite straight talk and contrary viewpoints (though not just for the sake of contrariness, of course). Though no CEO likes to be told he's wrong or what to do, good CEOs swallow their anger and indignation and evaluate whether the other person has a valid point.

With external candidates, the board absolutely must seek the answer to the following question: *What are their motivations for looking elsewhere to be a CEO?*

Most people want to become CEOs at the companies they've been with for years. Why are they interested in leaving "home"? Is it because they've been passed over for the top spot and want to show everyone at their company that they made a mistake? Or are they just drawn by the prestige of another company, a larger one, the CEO title, or the salary? Or are they truly eager to lead a specific organization as much as or more than their own? Asking these questions gives boards tremendous insight about a candidate's motivations and helps them see past a given individual's charm and reputation. In other words, it helps them determine why a given person is available. I have approached numerous prospective candidates who declined my overtures on behalf of a client company because they were confident that they were on the succession track of their current organizations.

Once a candidate is selected, the CEO must sit down and have the most open work discussion of his life. It means that the CEO must tell the candidate the following:

- What he would have done differently if he had it to do all over again
- An analysis of pitfalls in the company's strategy
- The areas where one should move quickly and where one should be cautious
- An evaluation of all board members, including information about who will help the new CEO and who might hurt him
- An assessment of the management team

Finally, the departing CEO needs to be brutally honest about his role in retirement. For instance, one retiring CEO told his successor something along the following lines:

I'll always be around to help you, but you should know that some of my people are probably going to go around you and come to me if you make an unpopular decision. If you're doing your job right, this is going to happen. I want you to know that I'm not going to respond to their complaints, so don't let this prospect impact your decision making. Even if you have to fire someone who worked closely with me for years, you should fire them; I won't interfere. And if I don't like when you're doing something contrary to the way I did it, I won't go to any board member to voice my complaints. This is now your company, and you can call me whenever you need my counsel.

Certainly CEOs face a challenge in keeping all these relationships straight. What helps is that each of the other four players in this dynamic has relationship responsibilities to the CEO. As we'll see, if the other four players are performing their roles properly, the odds increase that the CEO will keep the dynamic in balance.

Chapter Five

Boards

Selecting with the Shareholders in Mind

Sam Kinney, board member, Largesse Corporation:

I've served on other boards, but being a director for Largesse Corporation is the ideal. For one thing, my friend Jack is the CEO, and he knows how to treat his directors. It's not just that I receive a $100,000 annual retainer from the company and a separate consulting contract. It's that I'm treated with respect. Jack ferries me as well as the other directors back and forth to meetings in the corporate jet, and the annual board retreat in Hawaii with spouses is first class all the way.

I have to be honest and admit that when I retired as CEO of Mega Corporation two years ago, I missed that respect and found that I didn't really have an identity. More than one person asked me, "How do you keep busy, Sam?" and when I walked into the club, I know people were whispering, "That's Sam, the former chairman of Mega; I wonder what he's doing these days."

Being on the board of a Fortune 500 company has made me feel valued. I know Jack counts on me, and he recently asked me to chair the CEO succession committee. Our relationship goes back to Harvard Business School, where we both earned our M.B.A.'s. Over the years, we've maintained that relationship; we both have winter homes in Mountain Lake and our wives are friends.

Certainly there are times when I wonder whether Jack and I lean on each other too heavily. I know I'm serving Jack more than I'm serving the shareholders, and sometimes that bothers me. Though I'm going to head up the CEO succession committee, I'm pretty much in the dark as to the type of CEO who is best suited to lead the company in the coming years. Jack pretty much shields the board from a lot of strategic detail and what we do receive is filtered through him. It really doesn't matter that much, since the succession committee is pretty much a rubber stamp. Jack's COO, Jerry, is his choice to take over. My initial gut reaction was that Jerry isn't right for the job, but I trust Jack when he says Jerry is the guy. It would be great if we had other internal candidates to evaluate or if we could interview some outside people just for comparison's sake, but we have two years until Jack hits the mandatory retirement age of sixty-five, so there's no real rush to do anything now. If for some reason Jack sours on Jerry, we have plenty of time to find someone else.

At our last board meeting, Jack asked us to consider making him nonexecutive chairman when he retires in two years. On one hand, that makes me a little nervous, since I remember the stories Jack told me about how when he became CEO, the former CEO was on the board and looking over his shoulder, and how it prevented Jack from leading the company where it needed to go. On the other hand, I just know that Jerry is going to need help, and having Jack on the board for five years after he retires will make sure the company stays on course. Some of my fellow directors may grumble a bit about Jack's request, but they're all beholden to Jack in one way or another, and I'm sure I can convince any dissenters to go along with the majority.

CEOs tend to create boards of buddies. They fill them with people like Sam and establish a system of "you scratch my back and I'll scratch yours" that often fails to take shareholder concerns into consideration. This buddy system can create a fatal flaw in the CEO selection process by unbalancing it to the point that there is no systematic discussion and debate about the qualifications for the next CEO and no real effort expended to search for, interview, and select the best candidate.

Certainly there's a fine line between a quiescent board and a conscientious one. The latter should have a good working relationship with their CEO, respect his recommendations, and follow his lead in certain matters. It's natural that a friendship would evolve under these circumstances. But there is a line that both the CEO and board members should acknowledge, a line that determines whether they'll do a good or bad job choosing the next CEO.

A good board member works for the shareholders. A bad board member works for the company. A good board member is willing to ask provocative questions about succession and strategy. A bad board member only asks innocuous questions and lets the CEO be his primary source of information. A good board member neither tells the CEO what to do nor follows his orders but finds a middle ground where he fulfills advocacy and governance requirements. A bad board member pretends to put the shareholders first but picks up on the subtle and not-so-subtle cues of the CEO and follows them.

Whether board members are good or bad often depends on the incumbent CEO. The psychologically healthy CEO wants board members he can trust. The psychologically unhealthy CEO wants board members he can influence.

In certain ways, boards pose more potential problems than the four other players in our CEO selection dynamic. Part of the problem, of course, is that we're dealing with a group of people rather than one individual. But the problem also involves divided loyalty: How can a board member who owes his directorship to the incumbent CEO make a selection decision that is in the best interest of the shareholders but not in the best interest of the CEO?

The first place to start solving these problems is by striving for a truly independent board.

Independent in Thought and Deed

What constitutes an independent board? The Securities and Exchange Commission and U.S. Treasury Department don't consider directors independent if they act as advisers, consultants, or lawyers for companies on an ongoing basis or receive compensation in any capacity other than as a director. The cynic might respond that this just about eliminates everyone. In reality, independence isn't guaranteed by this definition, and I've seen many so-called "dependent" directors demonstrate highly independent thinking.

Although dependence can be financially based, and it would a big mistake for the majority of outside directors to be paid advisers, the real issue is misplaced loyalty. It's logical to assume that board members feel beholden to CEOs who appoint them to their boards. It's also logical to assume that board members often have or develop close friendships with the CEOs of the companies they serve. Many CEOs foster dependence through their proprietary feelings about boards. In recent years, I and other search consultants have become increasingly involved in recruiting board members, and more than one CEO has said to me, "I don't know why we need to involve a search firm to find board members, since it's my responsibility to appoint people to *my* board."

In 1999, the executive search firm Korn Ferry conducted a study and determined that approximately 18 percent of new outside directors were recruited by search firms. According to Peter Crist, head of the firm's board-search practice, that number was closer to 50 percent for the year 2000. Still, CEOs and the "old boy" network of current board members are responsible for bringing in the majority of members. It's not necessarily a bad practice for board members to recommend people—often current and former CEOs—who they believe would be great additions to the board. Board members are often in a position to bring in people with tremendous experience and expertise. The drawback, of course, is that they're often the same type of people. The diversity necessary for a modern board—women, minorities, people with international business experience, young dot-com entrepreneurs, and so on—are often missing when CEOs and established board members do the recruiting. What's also missing is an independent mind-set, a diversity of perspectives and ideas, that is crucial to the CEO selection process.

To help organizations recruit and maintain independent boards,

I've created two sets of questions. The first set is designed to ensure that there is a reasonable degree of financial independence and the second set to determine whether there is sufficient independence in thought, experience, and expertise:

Questions About Financial Independence

1. Does your board have an outside controlling shareholder?
2. Do board members' companies have business relationships with your company?
3. Do more than 50 percent of outside directors also serve the company in a paid advisory capacity (lawyers, consultants, venture capitalists)?
4. Do your board members sit on each others' companies' compensation committees?
5. Do your board members receive significant perks because of their membership (benefit packages, business steered to directors' firms, corporate charitable contributions steered to their favorite charities)?
6. Do your board members receive more than $100,000 in compensation?
7. Do your board members own stock in the company?

Charles Elson, head of the University of Delaware Center for Corporate Governance, states: "The cornerstone of my personal model for strong corporate governance has been director stock ownership. Equity ownership aligns the directors' interest with those of the organization and its shareholders, *rather than management,* and creates a kind of management monitoring vital to continued corporate success" (emphasis in the original).

I find it more than a little disturbing when I review proxies of a client company in which I own stock and learn that I own more stock than some of their directors!

Questions About Practical Independence

1. Have your long-tenured board members kept current (or do they share the same, traditional perspective)?

2. Are board meetings merely an audience for the CEO's presentations or do they address an agenda for difficult questions that challenge the CEO?

3. Is the composition of the board sufficiently diverse to address the organization's strategic needs (e-commerce, global issues, and so on)?

4. Does the board have an outside lead director?

5. Is there at least a significant minority of directors who haven't been the CEO's social friends for years?

6. Do your directors meet privately (without the CEO present) at least once a year to evaluate senior management?

7. Does the board include insiders other than the CEO?

8. Have many of the directors served on the board for more than fifteen years?

9. Are there term or age limits?

10. Does the former CEO sit on the board?

There are no definitive answers here. Ultimately, the answers come from what the board does rather than what it is. I've seen directors who were close friends of the CEO and paid advisers to the company challenge a CEO's choice to succeed him; I've also seen powerful CEOs turn supposedly independent directors into yes men. From my own personal experience, I've sat on the board of UCCEL Corporation, where the CEO was my friend, and learned how difficult it was to speak up and challenge the CEO's positions. What helped was that this CEO wouldn't have had it any other way and encouraged my independence. It would have been much more difficult if he had discouraged it.

Harry Bruce, former chairman of Illinois Central Corporation and author of a book on corporate governance, describes a board member's fiduciary responsibility as involving both "duty of loyalty" and "duty of care." The former means being loyal to shareholders above all else and especially above financial self-interest or friendship with the CEO. The latter refers to taking care that all one's actions as a director are above reproach and caring enough to ask the tough questions and challenge the CEO's decisions when necessary.

Keeping these two principles in mind helps directors who often must operate in gray areas. Too many situations have no clear path. Should a director vote to give a big contract to another director's company when it makes good business sense? Should a director vote for a merger that will provide him with a short-term cash windfall but that may not be in the best long-term interests of the shareholders? Should a director rubber-stamp the incumbent CEO's choice as his successor?

Directors have a legal safe harbor called the *business judgment rule* that protects them from shareholder lawsuits if they can prove they acted in good faith. They can make mistakes as long as they're not guilty of negligence or fraud. The problem, of course, is that many directors use the business judgment rule as a shield and make decisions that display a lack of independence. After all, many directors are beholden to CEOs because of lucrative board fees, extra benefit packages, profitable business steered to their firms, and donations made to their favorite charities. They also may feel as though the CEO is a great friend and may find it easier to place their loyalty to the CEO, whom they know, above their loyalty to shareholders, whom they don't know.

The point is that independence may be in the eye of the beholder. A director may truly believe that he is independent, though his actions say otherwise. In making your own determination as you consider the previous questions, I would recommend keeping in mind Harry Bruce's standards of *duty of loyalty* and *duty of care*.

The Ideal Board Member

Though it's important for boards to be diverse, individual board members should share certain traits that will make them valuable participants in the CEO selection process. If I were recruiting a new board member for an organization with an eye toward having her serve on the CEO succession committee, these are the traits I would want:

- Has an objective vision of where the company needs to go and what kind of leadership is required to realize this vision. *Objective* is a key modifier. This board member's vision isn't colored by personal bias about what defines a leader or an emotional attachment to the company's tradition. Instead, this ideal director makes it her business to understand the issues facing the organization, including the competitive environment, global threats and opportunities, and economic matters. This person recognizes whether the company's strategy needs to be maintained, tweaked a bit, or completely overhauled. Armed with this information, the board member demonstrates the courage of her convictions and makes it a priority to identify potential CEO successors who fit the corporate vision.

- Demonstrates a willingness to challenge the CEO on crucial issues. I'm not advocating board members who are obstreperous or contentious. I am, however, suggesting that ideal directors will respectfully but firmly bring up issues that may make the CEO uncomfortable, including those related to CEO succession and selection. These issues include

Convincing the CEO that it's time for him to leave

Proposing that CEOs' and key executives' pay packages be adjusted so they're more performance-based

Working with the incumbent CEO far in advance of his retirement to identify and develop possible successors

Challenging the CEO to consider outside candidates when he

insists that his successor will be the internal person he's mentored

Challenging the CEO to consider internal candidates when he insists that they recruit an outside "star" to be his successor

Refusing to allow the CEO to "hang around" long after he's retired; insisting that he not be allowed to have an office in the building or sit on the board

- Is willing to lead the CEO selection process rather than defer to the CEO. This takes gumption. CEOs often take the selection of their successor as an exclusive right, and a good director will politely but firmly disabuse them of that notion. If CEO succession requires going outside, it's time for the board to take over. This doesn't mean the CEO should be excluded from the process or even that he should take an inconsequential role. As discussed previously, however, the best role for the CEO is to allow the CEO selection committee to do its work and then participate as part of the team that interviews candidates and helps make the final decision. Volunteering to head the CEO search committee requires not only courage and the ability to tolerate some discomfort but also a lot of hard work. Some board members harbor the belief that being a director isn't supposed to be work, that work is what they do in their other job. Finding the right successor demands a lot of time-consuming phone calls, reading, and interviewing; it also requires a good deal of serious thought. The ideal board member, therefore, cannot be disinterested.

Besides these three traits for an individual member, the board as a whole must be diverse. This doesn't mean that every type of organization and functional area must be represented or that the board should be a rainbow coalition of different ages, ethnic groups, and gender. The ideal is a board of sufficient diversity that it can choose a new CEO based on a wide range of experience and expertise. At MassMutual, the selection committee included the chairman of a

Fortune 100 high-tech company, a former CEO and insurance entrepreneur, and an owner of several small businesses. Each of them knew something that was crucial for the selection process to turn out right. In fact, one of them had undergone the process as an internal CEO successor at his company. If they all had had similar backgrounds, they would not have had the capacity to choose the candidate they did.

There's a mistaken belief that the ideal CEO selection process is when the CEO and board immediately agree on the right candidate without debate or discussion. Though quick agreement on the right candidate is possible, it is more likely that such agreement signals that they've chosen the wrong candidate (probably the one the CEO has groomed for the job). Lively debates among selection committee members spark ideas that eventually produce the right specs for the job. Typically, each committee member starts out with their own favorite candidate, but by challenging each other, respecting everyone's viewpoint, and reflecting on the discussion, consensus usually is achieved. Remember, I'm not talking about acrimonious debate among young ladder climbers. Directors are usually highly intelligent, accomplished individuals who have learned to adapt and adjust their thinking for the greater good of the organization. They are less likely to adjust and adapt, however, if no one challenges their position.

Removing Obstacles to the Ideal

Before examining the methodology boards should use to select a CEO, let's think about why the ideal just described is rarely the reality. For instance, an ideal board would not have given departing P&G CEO Durk Jager a $9.5 million severance payment even though the company's value declined by $73 billion, or 50 percent, under his watch. Ideal boards wouldn't name CEOs to jobs and have to remove them less than two years later because they were unqualified to carry out their companies' strategies.

We've touched on some of the causes of less-than-ideal boards, such as the buddy syndrome. Although organizations don't control all the factors that result in boards delivering less-than-stellar performances, they can take a number of actions that will greatly increase the odds that boards will be independent, valuable contributors to the CEO selection process:

- *Compensate directors only with stock or stock options, based on company performance.* Organizations are moving away from compensating directors through salary, health benefits, retirement plans, and other perks. Paying directors as though they were management is absurd; they are not employees but independent outsiders. Stock compensation linked to company performance rewards directors for long-term success and profitability. In fact, a case can be made that all directors must own stock in the company whose board they sit on; some companies already require directors to own stock equal to more than three times their annual board compensation. This linkage between compensation and organizational success would motivate directors to take their CEO selection responsibilities seriously.

- *Encourage directors to leave who aren't ideal.* Admittedly, this is a touchy subject and one that even CEOs often don't want to deal with. But the fact remains that companies sometimes have deadwood on their boards and there is no method for getting rid of lifeless limbs. Or they have directors who are so obviously biased that they will throw the CEO selection process off kilter. Earlier I discussed the many signs that could signal a director was neither financially nor practically independent. Ideally, directors who lack this independence should be candidates for dismissal from their boards. But there are also clear behavioral traits that suggest a director should be dismissed, including:

Is inattentive in board meetings or constantly looks at his watch

Misses important committee meetings

Refuses to challenge questionable management ideas, ethics, practices, or plans

Votes consistently as the CEO wants him to vote

Is making a significant amount of money from his board membership fee, and needs it

Refers frequently to how things were when he was CEO

Sometimes CEOs can effectively rid themselves of unwanted directors by aligning themselves with respected leading outside directors and use their influence to encourage certain members not to stand for reelection. Perhaps the most opportune moment for a changing of the guard, however, is after a new CEO is chosen. Ideally, the retiring CEO will encourage his board loyalists to follow his lead and also depart the organization.

• *Make training a prerequisite for board membership.* It's frequently assumed that if someone has been a CEO, he's eminently qualified to serve on a board. This isn't necessarily so. Being an independent outsider is a radically new experience for some CEOs who may never have been independent or an outsider before. I remember when I recruited a top executive with a Fortune 50 company to serve on a board, and a few months after he'd joined the board, I asked the board chairman how he was doing. He said, "Well, his experience has proven invaluable, but one of us had to sit down with him and talk to him about all the voracious notes he was taking during meetings. Everyone knows directors don't take notes."

More significantly, directors need to learn stewardship and governance principles as well as certain CEO selection do's and don'ts; it's astonishing how many neophyte directors fail to realize that the board rather than the CEO is responsible for choosing the successor. The National Association for Corporate Directors can provide training in these areas. Their program should be mandatory for anyone who has never served on a board before.

• *Keep an eye out for corporate boardaholics.* I know some executives who sit on as many as twelve boards. They get hooked on sitting on friends' boards and are unable to satisfy their craving for being on bigger and better boards. As a result, they're stretched too thin and can't possibly devote the time and energy to matters such as CEO selection that they should—especially if they're also running a company as a CEO. As a general rule, no current CEO should be sitting on more than two outside boards, and no board member should be allowed to have more than five other board memberships.

- *Keep the board fit and fresh.* Stale boards choose stale CEOs. When many of a board's directors have served more than fifteen years, term and age limits don't exist, and directors all have roughly the same backgrounds and perspectives, stale thinking can be a problem. Boards that include a number of inside directors tend to manifest insular thinking. Boards that are too large (more than twelve directors) frequently experience difficulty obtaining full participation from all their members and allow a few people to dominate discussions.

Besides establishing limits on number of terms served, age, and number of members, organizations can keep boards fresh in a few different ways. One tactic to consider is looking beyond the known few (the professional board members) and tapping the many well-qualified chief operating officers, entrepreneurs, and experts in international and high-technology business. Some of these people may not fit the standard board member profile; they're not CEOs from established companies, they may be younger or a different color from the norm, they may not belong to the clubs or live in the areas of most board members. But they can infuse a board with fresh and at times unconventional thinking. Their voices may be crucial for choosing the next CEO, since they're more in touch with some of the issues the company will be facing in the next decade than other board members.

In addition, companies should establish specific criteria for selecting board members, evaluating their performance, and evaluating the composition of the board. Rather than talk about how the board needs to be more diverse or needs someone with a technology background, organizations must create evaluation plans and implement them. By continuously monitoring who is on the board and how effective they are, a company ensures that the people charged with choosing the next CEO are qualified for the job.

A Board's Selection Responsibilities

Although boards generally recognize their responsibility for helping choose their organization's next CEO, they don't always carry out all the steps that are part of this responsibility, or they don't carry them out properly. Let's look at the four basic steps and what they entail:

1. *Provide oversight for the succession process.* This step needs to be taken far in advance of the CEO's retirement. Early on in a CEO's tenure, the board must hold the CEO and chief HR person accountable for creating a pipeline of promotable executive talent and developing that talent. Too often, this pipeline doesn't exist or is poorly maintained, and when it comes time to look inside for CEO candidates, the selection committee comes up empty. Or even worse, they choose candidates without having a process in place that identified and developed people to become viable candidates. When this pipeline is established, the board should ask for annual reports from the CEO and HR chief about the succession candidates and their development. Further, the board should meet independently to review the outcomes. When it's time to start actively looking for a successor—or if the board decides the CEO isn't doing his job and needs to be replaced—three or four board members must be chosen for a selection committee.

2. *Become aware and involved in the organization's strategic planning.* This step takes place in tandem with the previous one. Boards should not wait until it's time to select a new CEO to oversee and approve the company's strategy. They should be briefed regularly by the CEO on the company's short-term and long-term goals and how the company plans to achieve them. Management should also present to the board at least once a year on a key strategic topic. Retaining an outside consultant, who would conduct strategic

audits every two years and integrate new challenges into the CEO performance requirements, might also be wise. Another useful approach is holding board meetings at the company's different sites, rotating from one location to the next so that boards can become familiar with the "guts" of the company and also get to know heads of office who might be prospective CEO candidates. I've seen too many boards that adopt isolationist policies simply by scheduling meetings off site and never getting down to the nitty-gritty issues that will determine the company's future. Without this knowledge, boards probably won't get the CEO specs right. Only when they're tuned into the company's direction can they figure out what skills and knowledge the next CEO requires to lead the company in that direction.

3. *Establish strong relationships with the other individuals involved in the CEO selection dynamic.* I've already discussed the importance of healthy CEO-board relationships in which the latter isn't dominated by the former. For the dynamic to balance properly, boards must hold CEOs accountable and challenge them at times. If they don't, and if a CEO is not comfortable in his own skin, the dynamic will probably become unbalanced and an unwise choice of a successor will be made.

Similarly, boards should carefully assess the company's HR chief and make sure he's a qualified and contributing member of the dynamic. HR chiefs who contribute the most are ones who are well-rounded; they are technically skilled in diverse areas such as labor, compensation, management issues, development, and the latest trends and techniques. For instance, HR heads can play critical roles in designing a compensation and benefits package for a prospective CEO that will be appropriate and enticing rather than inappropriate and a deal-breaker. Good HR chiefs are totally apolitical, possess a strong philosophical core, know how to use power wisely, and are superb lateral influencers. They are willing to challenge their CEO on issues of ethics. Boards must be alert for HR heads who are furnishing a false set of specs. In some cases, HR chiefs will create a spec sheet that doesn't reflect sound strategic thinking and may merely reflect a CEO's biases for a successor. Rather than accepting an HR chief's recommendations without question, boards must examine these recommendations with a critical eye. It's unfortunate that too few HR chiefs know how to develop a CEO spec.

Boards frequently have tenuous relationships with search consultants, in part because they view consultants as "bad news"; that is, if a search consultant has to be brought in, something is wrong. As a result, board members are often quite circumspect around consultants, refusing to provide them with sufficient information or treating them as unthinking purveyors of a simple service (the fetch-me-a-CEO mentality). Search consultants contribute the maximum amount to the search process when they have access to information. They become insiders. When I conduct CEO searches, I love nothing more than a board member who confidentially levels with me about the challenges the company faces, his own lack of knowledge, or the divided opinions among board members.

The key in the relationship between board members and prospective CEO candidates is openness, honesty, and involvement. In more than one company, board members choose from among the CEO candidates based on appearance and intuition. They rely on the fact that candidate A has a Harvard M.B.A. and has held a star position at a leading company to make their decision. Or they base their decision on how a candidate presents himself. What they don't do is get involved in the process, insist upon brutally honest conversations with candidates in which they express their doubts and hopes, and question candidates in detail about how they dealt in the past with situations that relate to the specs.

4. *Facilitate the transition from one CEO to the next.* When they arrive at their selection decision, the board must do whatever is necessary to ensure that the incoming CEO has the best possible chance of succeeding. Though this can mean everything from providing informal advice to suggesting useful resources, the main

responsibility is ensuring that the outgoing CEO plays the right role. The board must have a frank discussion with their outgoing chief executive about the role he expects to play once the new CEO is on board, as well as the board's perception of that role. Ideally, they'll be able to work out a mutually agreeable definition that will provide the new person with maximum support. If it seems as though the incumbent CEO intends to hang around indefinitely, however (he wants to keep his office, to be on the board for the next five years, use the jet and so on), the board has to take action.

Chapter Six

Search Consultants

Seeking the Long-Term Fit
Versus the Short-Term Fix

Ted First, executive search consultant and partner in McElroy, Roth & Associates:

When the chief HR executive at Largesse Corporation called me to do a CEO search, I wasn't surprised. Jack, their CEO, knows that I've handled assignments for some of his friends at other large corporations, and I'm sure he told their HR chief to give Ted at McElroy, Roth a call. Even without that connection, the odds were good that a company like Largesse would give our firm this assignment. After all, we're growing at a double-digit rate, we're among the largest of the global search firms, and we've received a ton of publicity for our high-profile CEO searches. We've taken some flack for this publicity, but there's no way the Wall Street Journal's "Who's News" section is going to mention you if you don't give them an exclusive about a completed search. The rules of the search game have changed, and we're making the most of it. Although we may not be able to give our "smaller" clients top partner attention anymore or handle unique, time-consuming searches, we're becoming the firm of choice for the world's largest corporations. We're a public company, after all, and that means we have to focus on our profits; that's why we're always looking to book assignments and close them as quickly as possible.

This Largesse CEO assignment is exactly the type of search we need. It's low-hanging fruit. Their HR executive told me that the point of the search is to balance outside candidates against internal people and that they'll pay the full search fee even if they go inside. I don't have to interview internal candidates or board members, though I am invited to the dinner at the Links Club with Jack, the CEO, and Sam, the head of their board's CEO selection committee. From what I hear, Jerry, the internal candidate, is likely to get the job. I realize that the situation isn't really fair for the outside candidates I recruit. But we recycle these candidates anyway, and I can just dig into our files to come up with an impressive candidate slate.

At times, I wonder about this business. I'm working like a madman with fifteen assignments, and I'm running my four associates and three researchers into the ground. On top of that, I'm competing with many of my partners for the same small body of talent. If we didn't have a central bank of candidates to draw from, we'd never be able to handle the workload. There have even been times when I've presented one candidate to more than one client. I'm not proud of this practice, but it's necessary. Besides, it's getting close to the end of my quarterly performance bonus, and I need the billings. I probably shouldn't take on this search, and in an ideal world I would not, but this isn't an ideal world.

The role of the search consultant in the CEO selection process is often misunderstood. Not only do organizations misperceive this role but so do many search consultants themselves (Ted being a prime example). The search consulting industry has evolved in ways that sometimes prioritize a short-term fix over a long-term fit. A recent article in the *Wall Street Journal* was headlined "High-Tech Recruiter Beirne Faces Sticky Issue of Fit," and it documented a star search consultant who had brought in people for top positions at companies such as America Online, Xerox, and Pointcast only to see them leave shortly thereafter. The article illustrated how difficult it has become to recruit the right CEO for high-tech companies. Similarly, there's a growing controversy over search consultants who practice "parallel processing," shopping the same CEO candidate around to different clients. And of course, the book-and-bill mentality of many large search firms has had a huge impact on how organizations view the industry. These large firms are "blocked" from recruiting from their numerous client companies and thus are denied access to many prospective candidates.

To make significant, positive contributions to the CEO selection process, CEO search consultants and their clients—the board of directors—must go about their task in a thoughtful, patient manner. The following section will suggest how it's possible to do just that.

Keeping One Eye on the Client and the Other on the Candidate

When I was starting out in the search profession at the consulting firm of A. T. Kearney, one of my mentors, Harvey Stenson, told me that I just had to remember two things: "Find a wonderful candidate for your client. And number two, find a wonderful career opportunity for your candidate." As I soon discovered, meeting both objectives was not as easy as it sounded. Then as now, CEO searches can veer off track for all sorts of reasons, including sacrificing the candidates' interests for the sake of the company's (or vice versa). Things start going off track when search consultants take shortcuts or fail to address key issues or when clients place unreasonable demands on the search process. To avoid these possibilities, search consultants must adhere to a comprehensive and balanced approach, as outlined in the following eleven steps.

Gain Some Essential Knowledge Before You Get Started About What Catalyzed the Client's Call

Obviously, you got the assignment because you or your firm received a call from a company that is interested in searching for a new CEO. But it's important to understand the specific dynamic behind the call, including who is the driving force behind the search, as well as its context and subtext (there may be events and issues surrounding the search that aren't stated up-front).

The initial call may be from a board member who is chairing the search committee, from the CEO who is about to retire and is looking for a replacement, or from the chief HR officer. A board member may call because the board is in the process of assessing the incumbent CEO and wants to hedge its bets; it's also possible the board and CEO have had open discussions about succession and are ready to launch a search. The CEO may call at the behest of the board, or he may be acting without the board's knowledge (a dangerous gambit). Some CEOs call search consultants just because they're contemplating leaving and they want to bounce some ideas off an objective third party. An HR chief may call because either the board or CEO requested he do so.

Given the many potential reasons for the initial call, it behooves the search consultant to understand the environment. Consultants in a rush to book a search may overlook an important search context that can doom their efforts from the very beginning. Here are some common preexisting factors that hurried search consultants overlook:

- *The search has been launched before the CEO agrees it's time to leave.* In other words, the CEO and board have not reached an agreement on the timing of the succession, but the board has decided to start the process in any case.

- *The CEO is reluctant to relinquish authority.* Although the CEO may have agreed to the search, he's dragging his heels. As a result, he will probably find something wrong with every candidate presented and may even refuse to step down when the board agrees upon a successor. Consultants who see this reluctance from the very beginning are asking for trouble if they conduct this search.

- *The search is for due diligence purposes only.* CEOs with no intention of leaving sometimes initiate due diligence searches to satisfy directors or "threaten" inside candidates. In essence, search consultants who participate in these searches are participating in a charade.

- *The CEO and the board haven't agreed on the specs for the position.* The search is going forward with board members and the incumbent CEO having very different ideas about the qualifications for the new CEO. At some point, there's going to be a whopper of a showdown, and the search consultant and lead candidate will be caught in the middle.

It's virtually impossible to recruit a good CEO under these circumstances. Participating in an uninformed search hurts the consultant's reputation, his standing with the candidate he recruits, and the company itself. As I became a more experienced search consultant, for instance, I learned to avoid many COO searches because hidden agendas were often involved.

From the very beginning, search consultants should consult! They should study the environment and offer advice to their client that can lead them to selecting the right CEO successor. If something seems "off"—if the search consultant perceives that a company isn't ready to start a search, the CEO and board are working at cross-purposes, or the search is a charade—he needs to call a time-out and talk to the client about his concerns. If these concerns aren't resolved to his satisfaction, he must be prepared to walk away from the search.

Unfortunately, some search consultants are neophytes at CEO searches and have great difficulty recognizing how and why they were hired (or they don't want to "take on" the client and ask the hard questions). They miss the subtext and context and move forward when they should screech to a halt. With the benefit of hindsight, we now know that the initial AT&T COO search should never have been conducted; the real solution was to replace the incumbent CEO with a new one. In other instances, the swamped senior search consultant hands off the search to a less experienced associate, who has never conducted a CEO search. Although the senior partner promises to work with him, this partner too often is involved in other work and the less experienced person blunders forward, oblivious to ominous signs. Clients are not always aware that this is the case. I once referred a CEO search to a large search firm partner who assured me that he would personally handle the assignment; I learned later that a junior associate was handling all initial contacts and interviews with candidates.

Define the Job

Some search consultants describe the CEO position requirements with definitions provided by the board, incumbent CEO, or HR chief. This is where CEO searches may start going in the wrong direction. It's not that organizations are unable to identify require- ments; it's just that they often don't put enough thought or analysis into it. Sometimes the problem is that companies are too close to the situation and can't objectively analyze what is needed. I've also seen board members who routinely accept the CEO's specs. And there are instances where the company simply hasn't done its homework but has relied instead on assumptions about require- ments that frequently are erroneous. In addition, some board mem- bers respond to a request for specific information about where the company is headed by saying, "We don't have a strategy. The new CEO has to develop it."

Search consultants, therefore, should conduct a situational analysis at the very beginning of the process. In fact, the process shouldn't begin until everyone is on the same page regarding the specs. Even if they receive a situational analysis from their client, they should take steps to verify it. People tend to forget that the executive search profession grew out of the management consult- ing business. Years ago, the setting of executive search requirements was preceded by an organizational study that examined both inter- nal and external issues. Only after such a study was done were exec- utive requirements set. Today, many search firms don't offer to perform this assessment or lack the capacity to do it.

To start the process effectively, therefore, consultants should conduct one-on-one discussions with the CEO and all board mem- bers. These discussions provide the forum for straight talk, which often is more difficult to achieve in a group setting. Search consultants need to emphasize to board members the seriousness of this endeavor, and remind them that they'll have to live with their choice long after the consultant and incumbent CEO are gone. It's not that boards don't recognize the importance of this selection task; it's that they sometimes assume it's a relatively easy chore that doesn't require research, analysis, reflection, and discussion. Worse yet, most board members are neophytes about CEO search or succession. In reality, a protocol for assessment of the CEO's role is the only way to make sure that the board meets this difficult challenge.

On a general level, the search consultant should ferret out information about the company's strategy, where the company needs to go in the future, and the qualities and experience required in a CEO to take the company to that future place. Based on this information, search consultants can gain congruence from the board and help their clients further crystallize criteria for CEO qualifications.

The following is a good outline for arriving at these qualification criteria:

I.   Identify company's needs on several fronts
   A. Corporate strategic direction
   B. Future business environment and competition
   C. Future organizational needs and cultural requirements
   D. Financial and competitive environment

II. Describe personal competencies and behaviors
   A. What candidates must have done (not just what they have said)
   B. Desirable personal competencies (initiative, judgment, courage, integrity, and so on)

III. Characterize critical leadership behaviors
   A. Vision, values, and energy
   B. Strategic driver skills, external focus
   C. Team effectiveness
   D. Organizational agility
   E. Motivational and risk profile

IV. Specify experience and educational requirements
   A. Specific industry experience
   B. Need for technical expertise

Consultant Don Baiocchi developed a less formal way of addressing CEO specifications by seeking answers to the following six questions:

1. What are the company's best future opportunities?

2. What are the company's most serious and immediate issues?

3. What are the company's current strengths and limitations?

4. What challenges should the company's new leadership address?

5. What attributes would you like to see in the CEO?

6. What are your thoughts on leadership succession in the company (especially the role of the incumbent CEO)?

Some search professionals might scoff at this detailed, time-consuming approach to the process or come up with a different set of questions. Like Ted, the search consultant working with Largesse Corporation, they might simply skip all of the above, delve into their files, and pull out the names of a number of potential candidates who they believe are qualified for just about any CEO position. But the right fit is difficult to find unless the job is defined up-front in all its complexity. A search consultant is responsible for leading the process so that he and the board can arrive at the appropriate specs. In addition, this up-front analysis prepares search consultants and members of the selection committee to interview potential candidates from a position of strength. They not only can assess candidates based on an intimate understanding of the client company's needs, but they can also attract these candidates with their perceptive analysis of how a candidate might be uniquely qualified to meet this company's CEO requirements.

One final aspect of the process must be defined up-front: the client contact for the search consultant during the course of the engagement. If this contact is not a board member, consultants should consider walking away from the assignment. For consultants to do a good job, they need to establish a strong, continuous relationship with the person or people who are empowered to select the next CEO.

Identify the Candidates

The common misconception is that this is the most difficult step, and some search consultants sell their ability to find the one perfect CEO out of millions of possibilities. But not only is the concept that there is one perfect CEO flawed, but the actual number of potential candidates for any CEO position are fewer than you might expect. Only about twenty thousand people occupy CEO, COO, group executive, or division president positions in the United States (the pool from which most CEOs are chosen). When you limit the search to executives with specific experience or in a certain industry, you often are dealing with a pool of hundreds rather than thousands. Typically, I'll look at anywhere from one hundred to three hundred potential candidates at the start of a CEO search. For the CEO successor search for Citicorp (before the Travelers merger), I started with a global list of 1,553 people in fifteen business sectors, the most I've ever looked at. The fewest I've looked at was thirty people for Ambrosia Chocolate Company's CEO search, since the candidate had to be a CEO or COO with experience in a specific industry, and there were only fifteen companies in this industry. In most cases, narrowing down the field is not a particularly difficult assignment.

The skill at this step is using thorough research, experience, and intuition to identify candidates who are not only qualified for a particular CEO position but are also likely to be interested in the job. For instance, a savvy search consultant knows that if the CEO of a given target company is in his mid-fifties and the COO is only a few years younger, that COO will probably be very interested in a new situation, since it's unlikely he'll become CEO at his own company any time soon. Similarly, a CEO of a $10 billion company will probably be receptive to opportunities to head a $30 billion company because it represents a step up. Or a young high-potential group executive may be stuck in a logjam. Former CEOs, too, may be interested in the position if they occupy nonexecutive positions or remain on boards. There are scores of clues like these that savvy search consultants recognize and act upon when identifying candidates. Search consultants should also examine what's been written about or by potential candidates and use this and other literature to include or exclude potential candidates. In our Internet age, enormous amounts of information are available on-line about the majority of prospective CEO candidates (this research was facilitated by the ability to access the EDGAR database on-line). Though this isn't true for other executive positions, most of the people search consultants look at for CEO positions possess sufficiently high profiles and have been around long enough that information about them is readily available.

The following steps are designed with absolute confidentiality and nondisclosure in mind. If you're involved in a public search, you obviously don't need to adopt the low-profile approach I advocate. Still, I've found that keeping searches confidential is a compelling objective for many companies, and the following is written with that objective in mind.

Review Prospective Candidates and Decide Whom to Contact

I usually begin by meeting with the chairman of the search committee to review the information gathered on prospective candidates and choose who to pursue. Some people are obvious choices, but others may be more difficult to make decisions about. It's also possible that the list is overly long. For these reasons, search consultants should help the client rank-order prospective candidates or at least divide them in to A and B lists. Spending more time gathering additional information about these people often is a good investment. Most search consultants know friends and former associates of people on these lists who can provide them with accurate preliminary assessments. Gathering additional data can avoid wasting a lot of time down the road on people who are not interested in the job or who are not qualified for it. Typically, a prospect list of fifteen to thirty potential candidates will be compiled during this step.

Approach Candidates

At this point, the search consultant's actions depend on whether the search is confidential. If it's not, the client company can and should be identified up-front. Most prospective candidates for CEO positions are wary of "cold calls." For this reason, I typically ship a package of client information overnight, including the specs, to the prospect's home and follow up with a phone call. In the majority of instances, however, the searches are confidential, and search consultants can't disclose client identity. Again, the following steps are written with confidentiality in mind.

The initial contact with a candidate involves sending him a position prospectus as well as information about the consultant. It's wise to send this information to the candidate's home rather than his office and call a few days later to determine interest. Sometimes I'll ask prospective candidates an open-ended question such as: *Is there any company that you're interested in more than others?* or *Are there any companies you wouldn't be interested in talking to?* Though the odds are against them naming the client company, it's a question that often yields informative answers.

After this initial contact, some prospects will drop out of the running. As the search consultant and client review the remaining prospects, they will determine who the consultant calls back and discloses the client to. If they are interested, I send them a hefty package with financial and strategic information about the company and then arrange to meet with them.

Meet Candidates

Although different search consultants have various approaches to initial meetings, I recommend in-depth, face-to-face meetings with the prospective candidates of up to three hours at a secure location. During this meeting, search consultants should share their knowledge about the client company, the personalities involved, and the requirements of the position. They should also assess motivation—why the prospect is interested—and whether he's qualified. Good search consultants view these initial meetings as a two-way street; they're not just thinking about assessment but also considering what it might take to convince a given individual to accept an offer.

After presenting the results of these interviews to clients, some consultants may conduct second interviews with some or all of the candidates. Part of the reason for the second interview is validation; questions often arise when clients and consultants review the results of the first interview, and this second session provides the opportunity to get these questions answered. In addition, consultants can use the second interview to set up the first meeting with the client, held usually at an off-campus location.

Bring Client and Candidates Together

The search consultant and the chairman of the search committee should select an off-campus site, usually a hotel suite, a room at a fixed-based operator, or a private club room. At times, I've arranged meetings at clients' or candidates' homes (including vacation homes). It's wise to take precautions to ensure the privacy of these meetings. For instance, more than one private search has become public because a company's private jet was noticed picking up a candidate for a meeting. All it takes is for a fellow business executive at an airfield to see the candidate, read the tail number of the private jet, and put two and two together.

The number of candidates interviewed can vary, but I usually push for clients to meet three to five people so they're exposed to different personalities and skill sets. The client and consultant should interview each candidate together.

Following each interview, the consultant and client fill out an evaluation form. After some time for reflection (usually a few days), they must make a decision about who to include on a list of semifinalists. The semifinalists are interviewed by the other members of the search committee, who also complete evaluation forms on the candidates. After the interviews are completed, the search consultant convenes a meeting of committee members to share results, impressions, and questions.

Normally, the committee chairman or a designated committee member conducts a second meeting with selected candidates. In addition, candidates will want to meet privately with the incumbent CEO.

Though there's room for a variety of approaches at this step, the one imperative is that committee members conduct multiple candidate interviews and evaluate them against a written set of criteria for the CEO position.

Make the Selection

Disagreement exists about the proper role of the incumbent CEO in selecting a successor. My belief is that this decision is the responsibility of the board of directors, no matter if the candidates are internal or external. Therefore, the incumbent CEO should be out of the picture until the selected candidates want to meet him. For their part, board members must avoid asking the incumbent CEO, Who would you pick? Although some boards allow the incumbent CEO to veto his successor, I don't agree with this practice.

Though a board selection committee will invariably cover a lot of ground during their discussion about the candidates, the consultant needs to make sure they address a frequently neglected question: Why is this person interested in leaving a top position with a good company? Many times, people simply assume that the answer is: Anyone in his right mind would want a shot at being CEO of our great company. Perhaps. But sometimes people are interested because they possess a flaw. For instance, they're never going to be CEO at their current organizations because they've been deemed to be a great individual contributor but a mediocre team player. Or they're interested in leaving because they've alienated too many people in their organizations. Certainly some people have perfectly acceptable reasons for wanting to leave: They're blocked from the CEO position because the incumbent will probably be there another ten years, or they lost out in a CEO horse race. Still, this is the time to answer this question and catch any flaws that might be lurking in their backgrounds.

At this point, the committee should decide who their selection is (or who their selections are—they could still have more than one at this point).

Vet the Candidate

Checking references remains a better-safe-than-sorry step. In most instances, search consultants who go through the previous eight steps can be reasonably sure that they've contributed to the process of choosing the right candidate. Still, there's always the possibility that something has been overlooked. Fetch-minded (rather than search-minded) consultants may check only three or four references and think their jobs are done. But consultants who take the process seriously recognize that it's worth the effort to be thorough. The key here is to verify that a client has made a good choice without "blowing your cover." This step normally takes place before any final offer is made, and confidentiality is paramount.

Candidates usually provide ample references, but I prefer to "reference the references" and make at least a dozen inquiries before I'm satisfied. Search consultants should have built a referencing base earlier in the process by contacting individuals who might know the candidates through business or even socially. At this point, it's wise to branch out if possible from the original reference list. In one search, our board members made it a point to talk to or observe prospective candidates at industry roundtables and other functions, thus gaining firsthand perceptions as backup to direct references. In most instances, however, using clients in this manner should be avoided because it can compromise the confidentiality of a search.

All sorts of ways exist, however, to vet a prospective candidate. A search consultant can disguise a reference conversation's purpose by saying the candidate is being considered for a seat on a client's board. Questions should focus on any significant spec issues or questions the search committee might have surfaced during interviews. Thorough networking can yield precious nuggets of information about most candidates.

What consultants should avoid here is asking a board member to do a reference check directly. More than once, board members have inadvertently let the cat out of the bag by asking someone who knows the candidate, "Just between you and me, we're strongly considering Nancy for our CEO. What can you tell me about her we don't already know?" On one of my searches, a candidate was fired by his CEO, who learned about his candidacy via a reference call from a client board member to one of his directors. CEO candidates can also be forced to make a premature decision about the job before it's even offered when their candidacy becomes public, a scenario consultants should guard against.

Negotiate

Negotiations can revolve around a number of points, but they usually involve the date-certain timing of CEO succession; compensation is the other common issue. Many client companies' boards retain outside compensation consultants or lawyers as part of this discussion. Search consultants are not experts in this area and shouldn't be asked to take on this role. Search consultants should be involved as a deal is negotiated, however, since they are the ones who have had the closest contact with candidates. Their presence isn't required because they're going to negotiate a great deal for their client but because they are still in the best position to attract candidates to the company.

In a real way, search consultants represent both the client and the candidate. The consultant has met with the candidate more often than the client and is attuned to the candidates' needs, compensation-related and otherwise. As a middleman in this negotiation process, the search consultant can and should advocate for the candidate. This advocating may involve emphasizing to the board that a given candidate will not tolerate the incumbent CEO staying on the board after a given period of time (or stating some other important condition), a protective covenant that facilitates a successful transition.

There have been times when I've spoken up during negotiations on behalf of a candidate, and a board member has turned to me and said something to the effect, "Who the hell are you representing?" I've responded, "I'm representing you by trying to attract this candidate appropriately. Here's what he wants, and if he doesn't get it, you won't get him."

Follow Up

Search consultants who, once the deal is done, never follow up by calling the successful candidate or the client are guilty of abandonment. After six or eight months of the new CEO's tenure, search consultants should make it their business to sit down with the person who hired the new chief executive (usually the board member who headed the search committee), as well as the new CEO, and see how things are going. Perhaps more than anyone else, the search consultant possesses the objectivity necessary to make an accurate assessment at this point. The consultant is the one both the client and the CEO are likely to complain to if something isn't going according to expectations, and the consultant can often intervene in these instances and suggest course corrections before things get too far off track.

Maximizing the Search Consultant's Contribution

On the most basic level, search consultants help organizations select their next CEO. The eleven-step process just described contributes to the larger selection process by facilitating the search from start to finish. But in a more important sense, search consultants contribute to the process by helping maintain the balance we've discussed throughout the book. Powerful people are involved in the search process, and it's easy for one of them to upset this balance purposefully or inadvertently. Search consultants, as the only "outsider" involved in the mechanics of the search, can provide perspective and objectivity that may otherwise be lacking. They can confirm the identification of candidate-profile criteria, compare internal and external candidates, protect confidentiality, and perform many other functions without bias or blinders. The CEO and board, certainly, have insights, experiences, and information that allow them to contribute to the search in ways search consultants can't. Sometimes, however, they don't take full advantage of search consultants for a variety of reasons. Let's look at some of these reasons as well as the ways companies can maximize search consultants' balancing contribution.

First, some organizations maintain that they don't need a search consultant to find a new CEO. Although there may be instances when they can function perfectly well without one, often they are deluding themselves by thinking they don't need outside assistance. Remember, most incumbent CEOs and board members are neophytes when it comes to CEO searches. Most have never had to conduct a CEO search or have only participated in such a search once before. A consultant who specializes in CEO searches has gone through the process many times and is aware of where the traps lie.

CEOs or boards that decide to go it alone usually rely on "old boy" networks. Typically, the board search committee or incumbent CEO doesn't take the process seriously and assumes that it's just a matter of talking to a few trusted people, receiving a few recommendations, and choosing between a group of equally qualified candidates. In these cases, organizations usually fail to make a good match between their strategic requirements and a candidate's strengths. A fast, simplified approach results in a "star" candidate who may look good on paper and present well but just isn't a good fit for the company. Often companies who select this way fall victim to the star syndrome, picking a candidate who seems to have sterling credentials. He may be someone who has received glowing reviews in the trade press or who has worked as the right-hand man for a superstar CEO. The problem, of course, is that accomplishments in one company don't automatically translate to accomplishments—or requirements—at another organization.

Second, organizations sometimes are reluctant to pay search consultants one-third or more of total CEO compensation for their services. Actually, there's some logic behind this reluctance. This compensation structure makes it in the consultant's best financial interests to find the most expensive candidate. When the consultant suggests to his client that they should offer him more money, the client's response often is, "Of course you're saying that, it will increase your fee." In fact, search consultants have coined a word that describes what happens when companies overpay their CEO choice. I've heard more than one consultant say, "I got a *write-up* on that assignment because they paid him more than they thought they would." In addition, one-third of total compensation can become a point of confusion and contention. What is total compensation? Base plus bonus? What about up-front money? What about stock options?

CEO search consultant Gerry Roche has proposed that a consultant's total search fee should be determined two years after the CEO candidate has been in office and based on increases in market capitalization, stock performance, or some other financial measure. As sensible a solution as this is to client complaints about excessive fees, it's not one that's likely to be implemented. Therefore, a flat fee makes sense, which is why my firm endorsed the flat fee structure more than twenty years ago. Though such a fee is usually a significant amount of money, it avoids the problems associated with percentage of salary.

Third, organizations sometimes have negative perceptions of search consultants because they had a bad experience with one in the past. There are search consultants who aren't good at what they do, but a bigger problem is choosing the wrong search consultant. It's a mistake to choose a search consultant because he is associated with a large, prestigious firm (or to choose one just because he's independent). Similarly, it's not a good idea to choose a search consultant because he's frequently mentioned in the business press (though you may want to hire his public relations firm).

A variety of search consultants exist with a variety of experiences, expertise, and styles. At the very least, your criteria for hiring one should include experience with CEO searches. It may also make sense to find someone who specializes in your industry, though there's a downside to this specialization: The consultant may not be able to contact certain industry people who are off limits because they work for client companies. Or they may have too many partners competing for the same talent.

If I were to choose a search consultant to help my company find a new CEO, my first two criteria would be an ability to have a dialogue with me on an equal level and an understanding of the dynamics of my company and industry. In other words, I'd want to find someone who acted like a business executive rather than a staff consultant, and I'd want his assurance that he personally would conduct the search. Next, I'd make sure that we could establish a level of trust and rapport that would facilitate our working relationship. To investigate these criteria, I'd ask the following questions:

- What is the most difficult search assignment you ever had?
- Can you tell me about a search assignment in which you failed?
- Will you provide me with the names of three or four CEOs or board members who can tell me about you?

- Can I contact three or four candidates you tried to place on searches (some of whom you didn't place)?
- What is your search process; what would be your first three steps?
- Are there any companies you can't recruit from?
- How busy are you; how many searches are you working on; do you have time to be involved in my search personally?
- How do you ensure confidentiality during a search?

In posing the last question, I'm reminded of the search wherein the retiring CEO told me: "If anyone calls me saying that they heard that I was searching for my successor, I'll deny it. Then, I'll call you to cancel the search." Happily, confidentiality was maintained and I successfully attracted Jim Hardymon to become CEO of Textron, Inc.

While there are no hard and fast answers to these questions, beware of search consultants who are too busy to be involved and intend to assign the search to a less experienced associate. Similarly, watch out for consultants who promise to find someone fast; this is a sure sign of a fetch mentality. A good sign is someone whose search process reflects some or all of the eleven steps described earlier; it suggests a thorough, well-thought-out approach to the search.

The best search consultants neither overstep nor understep their authority. For instance, they don't allow other people to get in between them and the decision maker. HR chiefs sometimes do get in the way by providing misleading information to search consultants or blocking them from the board or incumbent CEO. To do a good job, search consultants need to deal directly with the primary decision maker at the client. While HR people can be great partners in this process, they shouldn't "run interference" or block access.

From a purely ethical standpoint, good search consultants will not allow their client to hire the wrong person or permit a candidate to accept a job that will harm his career. In terms of the former, search consultants must sometimes stand tall and inform a board or CEO why their "favorite son" (often an internal candidate the CEO has mentored) may be the wrong choice, given the specs they've elaborated. In terms of the latter, the consultant should dissuade a candidate from accepting a CEO position that seems to be fraught with career peril. If the ground rules for succession have changed and the search consultant knows that the incumbent CEO has no intention of stepping down date-certain (despite his promises to the contrary) and that the candidate is going to be stuck in a COO position indefinitely, the consultant has to make all this known to the candidate.

Along the same lines, search consultants who truly contribute to this process will neither fetch candidates at one extreme nor make the final choice at the other end of the spectrum. This latter issue is critical. Search consultants should not point at a candidate and say, "He's the one." Instead, they should present options that the client decides upon. A good consultant will consider and compare the candidates on the slate and say, "Jane seems better for your organization from a cultural perspective and meets all the specs, though she's a bit weak in strategy. John also meets all the specs, though his leadership style may result in a culture clash."

Providing viable candidate options and exploring the consequences of each option is a tremendously valuable service. By ensuring that serious, objective analysis goes into the process, search consultants maintain the balance that is crucial to making the right choice.

Chapter Seven

The Candidates

Developing Savvy

Jerry Martin, COO, Largesse Corporation:

Some board members have told me that I'm their choice to succeed Jack, but they also have counseled patience. Jack, too, has indicated that my day would come but not to expect it in the near future. Though Jack won't admit it, he's probably going to remain in charge of things— whether as CEO or in a less official capacity—for another five to seven years. In fact, I know he's already had informal discussions with the board about naming him nonexecutive chairman. That means that if and when I become CEO, I'll be fifty-five years old and running the company with Jack looking over my shoulder. My wife thinks I'm nuts to stay, but I know Largesse inside and out and I think I can turn it into a global growth machine.

My other concern is that Jack is not preparing the company for a changing market, so that when I finally am in charge, I might not have the right experience or resources to take Largesse where it needs to go. What really worries me is that neither I nor any of our top people have significant international experience, but the overseas market seems as though it's changing to the point where we need to get into it. Two of our competitors have acquired European manufacturers, but Jack won't do the same, because it would be "betraying" his friendships with foreign distributors. I'd love to bring this up when I present operating results to the board, but Jack would kill me; he forbids anyone bringing up stuff like this to the board without his prior approval—approval he'd never give me.

On top of all this, I've been contacted by a search consultant who is looking for a CEO successor for a large international manufacturer. Their CEO is retiring and his board is looking for a successor. I've done the initial interviews and met the board, and they've assured me of their support. However, they've been very vague about the company's strategy, and the incumbent wants me to come in as COO for a year. The incumbent seems reluctant to put date-certain succession in writing, plus I have a feeling that the one-year COO period will be viewed as a test and that if I don't pass with flying colors, I won't get the CEO job.

Still, I want to be CEO, and it seems that the fastest way to do so is to take this CEO-successor position and leave Largesse. The CEO at the international company has promised me that after one year, he intends to retire and will sever all ties to the organization. He seems sincere, so I think I'll accept the COO position, if offered.

As both an internal and external candidate, Jerry is in a difficult position. Like many candidates, he is so eager to become CEO that he is willing to "suspend his disbelief" and naively accept the terms dictated to him. Rather than playing an active role in the selection dynamic, he is passive to the point that he upsets the dynamic's balance. At both Largesse and the international manufacturer, he refuses to assert himself and set reasonable conditions that would greatly increase his chances of being a successful CEO.

Part of the problem is that most CEO candidates are neophytes. Just as most boards and incumbents have never conducted a search for a CEO successor, most candidates have never interviewed or been selected for a CEO position. At the same time, these candidates are usually champing at the bit to become CEO. Internal candidates being considered for the spot are so nervous about doing something that might eliminate them from the running that they refuse to ask a question or set a condition that might hurt their chances. Instead, they may butter up both the incumbent and the board of directors in an attempt to win their favor. External candidates, too, may refrain from asking the hard questions and negotiating the conditions that will help them become effective CEOs. Fearful of losing the opportunity because they're getting a bit long in the tooth to be CEO or under self-imposed pressure to grab the brass ring (they're the only one in their group from graduate school who is not yet a CEO), they allow themselves to be talked into a deal that is unsatisfactory.

At the very least, candidates should gather their courage and ask some basic questions before accepting any CEO position. Let's examine what these questions are and why they're important.

Learning the Questions, Learning from the Answers

Although internal candidates may know more about the CEO position and the company than external candidates, both face sizable knowledge gaps they need to bridge. Bridging these gaps is necessary in part to inform them of whether they should accept an offer, but it's also critical in determining whether the fit is right. Questions can be asked about a variety of topics, but some of the more important areas are knowledge of the company, circumstances of the incumbent's departure, the company's succession plan, and compensation. Let's examine the questions one by one:

- *Why is the position really available?* This obvious question often goes unasked because candidates fear offending the selection committee by putting them in an awkward position (that is, having to admit they fired the previous successor they had selected). Prospective candidates must ask deep questions of the board (they will have been prepped by the search consultant). They can talk with the incumbent or deposed CEO as well as other executives currently or previously with the organization. It's important to discover whether the job is open as a result of a termination or resignation, as well as the circumstances surrounding the termination or resignation. Candidates might learn that the board terminated a previous CEO successor after a relatively short tenure in office or that the individual resigned because promises were not kept. They might also discover positives: The incumbent might tell a candidate that he is leaving because he's not up to the challenge the company is facing, but for someone with the right background it's a great opportunity.

• *What is the company's strategic business plan?* Candidates should receive proxy reports, analysts' statements, and formal strategic descriptions as a matter of course. If they don't receive these things, they should ask the search consultant or search committee head for them. They will probably be asked to sign a confidentiality agreement. If they are refused permission to look at them (once the search committee or consultant is at liberty to disclose the company's identity), they should walk away. Consider what it might be like to learn that the company's strategy is unrealistic or ill-conceived (at least in your opinion). Before accepting any CEO position, candidates should be well-versed in everything from the company's product lines to key customers to financials to industry outlook to strategic challenges and key competitors.

• *How did you develop the specs for the job?* The answer to this question can provide insight into the strengths and weaknesses of the organization. Search consultants as well as search committee members should be willing to explain how they established the criteria for the position, why this set of criteria was prioritized, and who participated in the process.

• *Why are no internal candidates being considered?* External candidates are entitled to ask this question for a number of reasons. First, it will tell them about the existing succession plan—or lack thereof. It's not a good sign if the board has failed to address this issue. Second, it will help them understand the logic of why they are prospective candidates; they can learn the reasoning behind their being contacted and can deduce whether they are indeed qualified based on that reasoning. Third, it will alert them to the internal political situation. Are there disgruntled internal people who were passed over for the job?

• *What characterizes the culture?* Gil Amelio may have failed at Apple because he couldn't grasp the culture (or he underestimated its power). Durk Jager may have failed at P&G because he steam-rolled the culture. Although the type of culture a company possesses shouldn't determine whether candidates accept or reject a job, understanding a culture can illuminate the real challenge of the job. Given this understanding, candidates can ask follow-up questions such as

Can I turn this legacy culture loaded with conformity and consensus into a more combative, performance-driven one?

Can this culture, characterized by hubris ("we are the best company in the world"), become more strategic and grounded in changing marketplace realities?

Am I going to learn about this culture and enhance it, or am I going to change it?

Will I have the capacity to change it?

Do I have authority to get rid of sacred cows (which embody the legacy culture)?

Will I have the board's support for cultural change, and will they support me if I want to fire a favored executive?

Will the retired CEO make a fuss if I start changing the culture, and will the board support me over him if this happens?

- *What is the agenda and timetable for succession?* This is a question every candidate must ask. When candidates fail to ask it, they jeopardize both the health of their organizations and their careers. Date-certain succession plans are essential, and it's a mistake to accept vague or verbal answers to this question. A side letter of agreement from the board (separate from the employment contract) should specify the plan and dates.
- *What are the incumbent CEO's plans once I come on board?* Candidates need to ask this question directly. They should avoid scenarios in which they're brought in as COOs for a trial period that may stretch for a year or more. In fact, incumbent CEOs who hover over their successors' shoulders do no one any favors.

Whether they're overseeing a COO or serving as nonexecutive chairman or a member of the board, their presence limits the CEO successor's effectiveness. In fact, CEO successors should negotiate agreements whereby they receive significant compensation if succession plans aren't adhered to. If an incumbent CEO doesn't turn over the CEO reins when he said he would, or if he breaks his promise to sever all ties with the organization on a given date, then compensation should be awarded to the wronged successor.

When candidates ask these questions, they make a great contribution to the process by securing information that assures them of a good fit with a given organization. Informed candidates are less likely than uninformed ones to thrust themselves into the running for a position that is ill-suited to their talents, experience, and expectations.

How Candidates Should Present Themselves

Candidates need to give search consultants and the search committee an honest and complete sense of who they are as individuals and professionals. Any distortion of this persona can result in an unbalanced process and cause boards to select candidates who are not as they appear. The problem, of course, is that a CEO position means so much to candidates that they sometimes are tempted to present themselves as who they think the search committee wants them to be rather than as they really are.

Though candidates naturally present their experience and expertise in a favorable light, they should not cross the line and exaggerate or lie in an attempt to impress. Unfortunately, I've encountered candidates who have attempted to deceive me and the client about their work experience and educational background. Dave was the CEO of a small company who was a candidate for my client's larger company. Orally and in writing, his credentials appeared impeccable. But when I vetted these credentials, I learned that he did not have the M.B.A. he claimed to possess on his company profile and in his biography in the proxy and 10-K. Dave was eliminated as a candidate when I made this discovery, but imagine the disaster if he had been selected as CEO-successor and had lied not only about the M.B.A. but about his skill at mergers and acquisitions. He would have been hired in the belief that he could manage a complex acquisition without ever having done one before!

Candidates who are comfortable in their skin are content to be themselves on paper and in interviews. At the same time, however, they should be aware of how important first impressions are during interviews with board members, who frequently make quick judgments. Jack Welch called these first impressions the "up-front hit," the initial impact made by everything from personal appearance to manner of speaking to body language. Search committees interviewing candidates frequently make a yes-or-no decision during the first two minutes. For this reason, I counsel candidates to make sure that they're fully informed about the company and that they ask three or four good questions that demonstrate their knowledge. Candidates who spend these precious opening minutes bragging about their accomplishments or taking a neutral, passive stance usually have no chance, no matter what they do during the rest of the interview.

My admonition to "be yourself" has to be taken with a grain of salt. Some candidates are eccentric or idiosyncratic; they may simply have an affectation or stylistic quirk that rubs board members or the incumbent CEO the wrong way. For this reason, it's wise to play it "straight" during these interviews, taking a middle-of-the-road stance in terms of clothing, speech, and so on. I once was handling a search in which the committee had decided on a particular candidate who seemed a good fit. To seal the deal, the candidate and his wife were invited to a golf tournament sponsored by the company. The plan was for the candidate to play golf with the chairman and board members and then for the offer to be made later that night at dinner. The next morning I called the chairman and asked him how it went, and he replied, "It's off." I asked him what happened and he said, "Can you believe the guy arrived at the first tee wearing a gold necklace under his golf shirt? No way we're going to hire someone who wears a gold necklace!"

Between the incumbent CEO and board members, you're likely to find one cranky old traditionalist who recoils at what he views as untraditional dress or behavior. He has a picture of a CEO in his mind, and if even a small detail of the candidate doesn't fit with that picture, the candidate is out.

The other presentation issue to keep in mind is the response to questions. I've heard candidates asked just about every question in the book (I've asked some of them myself), and the ones who answer honestly, thoughtfully, and concisely make the best impression. For instance, I often tell candidates that I believe people learn best through meaningful failure and ask them what was their biggest failure, why it happened, and what they learned from it. Candidates who claim they never failed are usually being dishonest. People who offer a minor failure as a kind of sop to the question demonstrate a lack of candor. Candidates who answer the question completely, however, provide evidence not only of their honesty but whether they learned from a particular failure.

For many years, I used to believe that the most important criteria for candidates was a sterling track record. More recently, I've come to the conclusion that behavior is more important than experience in deciding on a candidate. Once I presented a highly qualified candidate who was passed over for a CEO position because one of his conditions for accepting the job was the resignation of all board members. This demand was actually reasonable; the company was in a turnaround situation, and the candidate rightly felt that the board bore some responsibility for the situation. But this candidate's behavior alienated the board. He came across as arrogant and inflexible. Had he presented his case in a more flexible, less judgmental manner, he might have been selected and performed admirably. Unfortunately, his behavior deprived him of the chance of a terrific opportunity and the company of a leader who may well have been the best person for the job.

Internal Issues

Ideally, a company has a great CEO succession plan. The CEO, chief HR officer, and the board observe the performance and promotability of top people in a series of key jobs over a period of years and develop the candidates along the way. When the CEO is ready to retire, the best candidate has clearly identified himself by his performance, and the selection decision is obvious to all.

Unfortunately, this ideal scenario is uncommon. As I described earlier, CEOs often ask internal candidates to participate in a horse race that encourages executives to prioritize short-term results (which will impress the board and incumbent CEO) at the expense of long-term goals. These horse races are especially prevalent in Darwinian cultures where survival of the fittest is deemed an appropriate selection criteria. I once saw a documentary about how lions conquer territory. A young lion finds a lioness with cubs, kills the cubs, and then produces his own cubs with this lioness. This is how he generates his pride and becomes an alpha lion. Some CEOs do basically the same thing; they kill off their perceived successors (consciously or not) so that they can continue to maintain power because "my people aren't ready to take over." Internal candidates are encouraged by this culture to kill their competition. In fact, I've heard a board member say of a candidate, "He may have killed off his competition, but that just proves he's the best person for the job." Candidates in these types of environments are rarely the best people for the job. Instead, they're the most ruthless and most political.

Even if internal candidates are vying for the CEO position in healthier cultures, they still are at a disadvantage compared to external candidates. Once they are officially designated as a candidate, only two things can happen: They will be selected; they will be passed over. Most candidates feel tremendous anxiety in this situation, and their performance suffers. Unlike external candidates, they are emotionally invested in the organization and may have dreamed for years of becoming its CEO. As a result, before the selection is made, they go to work every day as a candidate rather than as an executive with a job to do. This pressure can take its toll and cause candidates to do things they might not otherwise do. Even the candidate who is selected for the CEO position may be willing to make concessions and agree to terms that he knows are not in his best interest or the best interest of the company, but he wants the job so badly that he is willing to agree to just about anything.

Finally, internal candidates often aren't trained to be CEOs. External candidates often have a range and depth of experience that better prepares them to take on a chief executive position. Not many companies have CEO training programs for candidates; they aren't developed over time so that they acquire the skills and knowledge necessary to lead the company according to its strategic plan. Even worse, many of these candidates naively assume that they are prepared because they've observed the CEO in action, sometimes for more than twenty years. As the selected candidate discovers, observation is no substitute for doing.

Negotiating the Deal

When a candidate is informed that he is the board's choice to be CEO successor, serious negotiation begins. If the selection process has followed our balanced ideal up to this point, the candidate must make sure he doesn't unbalance it by demanding too much or too little. In terms of the former, remember that our aforementioned candidate demanded that the entire board offer their resignations. Some candidates capitalize on their selection by requesting all sorts of perks—from luxury cars to chauffeured limousines to new corporate jets to family travel and vacations—that cause resentment and diminish their stature (and ultimately their effectiveness) right off the bat. At the other extreme, some CEO successors are so grateful for their selection that they refrain from insisting upon appropriate conditions—a succession timetable detailed in a side letter, consensus on the role of the incumbent CEO during and after the transition, and so forth.

At this point in the process, candidates should retain their own counsel to negotiate the deal. At the very least, they shouldn't sign an employment contract without third-party review. While some of the issues at this stage are standard, such as putting together an appropriate compensation package, others may be unique to the situation and require a good deal of thought and negotiation. One negotiation I was involved in resulted in a paragraph stating that if difficulties arose between the CEO successor and incumbent CEO, the board would give the successor 100 percent support. Of course I'm not intimating that a selection committee will be overjoyed when a candidate brings in counsel to help with the negotiation. I witnessed the chairman of a technology company ranting and raving when such counsel presented him with a list of requirements that he believed were unreasonable (in reality, they were quite reasonable and the board eventually met all the requirements).

As deals are being negotiated and finalized, more than one candidate has gotten cold feet and reneged after the offer has been accepted. In most cases, this is the worst thing a candidate can do, both in terms of his own career and for the organization that wishes to hire him. Typically, candidates renege because they have a variation of buyer's remorse: once they accept the offer or seem as though they have accepted it, the reality hits home and they have second thoughts that cause them to back out of the deal. In other cases, they tell their boss that they're going to accept the CEO offer, and their boss manages to persuade them to stay. One CEO told a resigning executive: "This isn't your boss talking; this is your best friend—you can't leave me right now." He flattered him and made him promises, and the executive agreed to stay. Within the year, he was looking again.

My advice to external candidates is make sure you're ready to make a move before telling a search consultant or search committee that you're a candidate. Ambivalence is not the proper attitude for candidates; this isn't a process you should enter into half-heartedly. I've found that a host of factors cause people to become candidates for CEO positions, including career blockage, relocation requirements, inadequate compensation, lack of recognition, discrimination, poor chemistry, glass ceilings, being passed over internally for the CEO position, and so on. These may be valid reasons to become a CEO candidate at another company, but it would be wise for these executives to determine whether the problems can be solved at their own organizations before they start looking elsewhere.

If you're a candidate who jumps prematurely and then reneges, you can expect a number of negative repercussions. First, you've embarrassed the hiring company and damaged your reputation, creating doubt about your loyalty and decision-making courage. Second, you've hurt yourself at your current organization because you can never be completely trusted again; you were willing to jump once so you'll be willing to jump twice (or so the reasoning goes). Third, you may have caused tremendous harm to the hiring organization. They may have spent months searching for the right candidate and now they have to start over from scratch. If they're in a turnaround situation or in desperate need of leadership for any other reason, you've dealt them a serious blow. The moral of this story is that reneging helps no one and hurts everyone.

Finding the Right Stance and Pace

Once new CEOs are named, they can still throw the process off kilter. When the announcement is made, a candidate is in the spotlight. Whether he's an internal or external candidate, he's being watched both by everyone who will work for him and by the board (as well as the previous CEO, if he's still around in some capacity). Regardless of whether he was a star at another company or has been home-grown, he is the focus of much speculation and expectation. An offhand remark or action can be blown out of proportion. For an initial period, the new CEO is viewed with a certain amount of caution. As much as the company may have wanted this candidate, there were other candidates who weren't chosen that the successor is compared to. If a CEO successor is named and the incumbent CEO is a powerful and visible presence, the scrutiny is even more intense. Until this successor proves himself, he is under the microscope.

For these reasons, CEO successors should proceed at a moderate pace. Of course, moderation is the last thing on many new CEOs' minds. From the moment they are named to succeed the current CEO, some people make sweeping decisions and issue edicts with lightning speed. Because they don't pause, gather information, and assess before doing these things, they often come across as imperious and egotistic. Whereas certain turnaround situations require swift action, the majority don't. However, new CEOs shouldn't be overwhelmed by their new stature and refrain from making any decisions. Perhaps anticipating a negative reaction if they try to change things too quickly, they adopt a passive, indecisive stance that is just as counterproductive as being overly aggressive.

When candidates become CEO successors, they should proceed with equal parts speed and caution; they should get a feel for the situation before moving forward. If it's a healthy situation and the incumbent is an ally and the board is 100 percent behind the successor, it's possible to move with greater speed. If the board has just gotten rid of the previous CEO, however, the new chief executive may want to take one step backward and then two steps forward. It's useful to gather the management team off campus and verify strategic issues raised by the board during the search and selection process. Private discussions with individual board members as well as the leadership team can be insightful and forge relationships that can serve the CEO well, especially during the first year. Although the new CEO may want to bring in his own people and ask veteran executives to leave, it's wise to embark on this hiring-and-firing phase gradually (and after a solid assessment of current executives has been undertaken).

Thoroughness, thoughtfulness, decisiveness, and humor are all attributes that stand a newly minted CEO in good stead. Finding a comfortable middle ground between inaction and overreaction is a reasonable strategy. If the process has been effective, the new CEO has been selected carefully, comprehensively, and objectively. It would be a shame to spoil this process at the last minute with rash decision making or no decision making at all.

Chapter Eight

Chief Human Resources Officer

Demonstrating Capacity of Influence

Mark Dunhill, CHRO, Largesse Corporation:

I've been the chief human resources officer of Largesse for fifteen years, and I came up through the company ranks. As the CHRO, I've always reported to our CEO, Jack, and I think it's fair to say we have a strong bond. That's why I feel a little funny about the call I received from one of our directors, the chairman of the compensation committee. He asked me to prepare a CEO succession plan for Jack's replacement in antici-pation of his retirement, and he wants me to present it at the next board meeting. He also wants me to bring in an outside consultant to do a management audit.

Jack has always discouraged me and other executives from interact-ing directly with the board, especially without his initiating the interac-tion. Even Jerry, our COO and heir apparent, isn't allowed much contact with them, and I'm not sure whether the board realizes that Jerry is Jack's choice to succeed him. That's why I went to Jack and told him about what the board director had asked of me. I was somewhat relieved when Jack told me to ignore the request and that he'd handle the board. What he wants me to do, however, is prepare a succession program that slates Jerry as the candidate. Apparently, Jack has been working with his good friend Sam, who's on the board, and he's made Sam the head of a CEO selection committee. His plan is for me to bring in a search con-sultant to generate candidates who can be compared to Jerry, but this is just for show.

I guess what bothers me the most about this whole process is that we might lose Jerry, who really is a good candidate for the job. The other day

I received a call from a search firm friend of mine, and he told me he received a call from the Wall Street Journal *telling him that Jerry was one of three candidates being considered for the CEO position at one of our competitors. I don't think Jack realizes that Jerry has options and is likely to take them. As much as I like and respect Jack, I think he's always been a bit too controlling, and Jerry resents this aspect of his leadership style. I remember at our annual shareholders meeting last year, a shareholder directed a question at Jerry about six-sigma and Jack spoke before Jerry had a chance to answer. Though Jerry didn't say anything about it, I could tell he was miffed. I'm sure he feels the same way about how Jack is orchestrating his succession. I just wish there was something I could do to prevent us from making a big mistake.*

CHROs like Mark are torn between loyalty to two masters, the CEO and the shareholders. Because they report to the CEO and often have established a close working relationship over the years, CHROs naturally feel loyal to their bosses. At the same time, the nature of the position is such that HR chiefs must work with and be accountable to boards of directors. In certain instances, such as CEO succession, they can be placed in difficult positions where they're faced with not sharing information with their CEOs and must work exclusively with the board. In these situations, more than one CHRO has reported that he feels as though he's "working behind the CEO's back." It's no wonder, then, that some CHROs choose to honor their loyalty to their CEO over their duty to the organization (after all, their jobs are at stake). As a result, they contribute very little to the CEO selection process and sometimes contribute negatively. Or if they try to please everyone all the time, they are doomed to fail.

While CHROs *can* play a significant role in this process, they usually don't. Sometimes they are the ones who decide to opt out, and sometimes others exclude them. In either case, their omission has contributed to the rash of CEO selection failures. Now more than ever, CHROs and their organizations need to step up to maximize the HR chief's contribution to the succession and selection processes. In addition, board members must meet independently with the CHRO to monitor the development and recognition of the executive pipeline for succession. One of the biggest obstacles to these actions, however, involves the CHRO's self-perception.

Two Very Different Self-Perceptions

Mark is typical of CHROs who basically view their jobs from a staff or administrative perspective. It's not that they're bad at their jobs. Far from it. Many of these CHROs handle policy issues well and make sure various functions operate efficiently. What they have trouble with is straight talk and taking a stand. They're unwilling to challenge the CEO, and they often aren't well-versed in business matters outside of HR. Some of the HR chiefs may want to be more involved in strategy or see themselves as being more than policy wonks and pencil pushers, but they can't get out of the box that their CEO has put them in. The CEO doesn't want to give them the responsibility that would allow them to be an integral part of the management team.

The other type of CHRO is as much a leader as any general manager. In fact, they resemble general managers in the best sense of that term. They see the big picture, are strategic, grasp business dynamics, and know the competition. They have a special relationship with the CEO, one that other top executives might not enjoy. As the person entrusted to create and maintain the company's development culture, he must work closely with the CEO. As the individual who will consult with the CEO about who internally is qualified to succeed him, he has a responsibility that is near and dear to the CEO's heart. This type of CHRO, however, doesn't let this relationship prevent him from talking straight with the chief executive. In fact, he feels this relationship makes it easier for him to tell the CEO how things are without worrying how it will affect his position in the organization. He is especially focused on building the organization's talent pipeline and takes his succession planning duties very seriously. Not only the CEO but also the board and other members of the management team consider the CHRO an equal and respect and request his insights. He would not allow the CEO to put him in compromising situations with the board of directors.

Perhaps the best phrase that describes this CHRO is "capacity of influence." Influence over CEO succession and selection decisions is something that an HR functionary—even a highly competent functionary—lacks. When this CHRO speaks, boards listen. He may not always exercise this capacity, since his role in selecting the next CEO is more limited than that of the board. However, this HR chief knows when it's appropriate for him to exert his influence and is perfectly willing to do so.

What's interesting is that both the influential and noninfluential CHROs may believe that they play significant roles in CEO selection. In a survey my firm conducted, 68 percent of the 350 CHROs surveyed said they were more involved in CEO successor searches than in the past; 89.5 percent attributed that increased involvement to their active membership on the senior executive team. Almost 78 percent indicated that they personally have been involved in CEO, COO, or board searches. But only 25 percent actually selected the executive search consultant! Most of the time, that decision came from the board or the CEO. I would suspect that today, these percentages have increased.

Although most CHROs view themselves as playing a key role in CEO selection, this perception doesn't always jibe with reality. Our firm's study also revealed that nearly half of all Fortune 500 companies surveyed lacked a formal, board-sanctioned CEO succession plan. One would think that more CHROs who are involved in helping their organizations find the next CEO would have created such a plan or boards would have requested one. Even assuming that some organizations have young CEOs or have an informal succession plan, it still is telling that only 50 percent have formal plans.

Most CHROs truly believe they're contributing to the CEO selection process, but this belief does not emanate from experience.

Most of them haven't had the chance to participate in this process in the past, so it stands to reason they find it difficult to assess what constitutes a significant role. We can help assess it by first looking at what CHROs can do to make sure the right internal candidates are identified.

Internal Fortitude

Even highly competent, highly experienced CHROs sometimes drop the ball when it comes to helping their organizations identify and select the appropriate internal candidates. Just the other day I had lunch with a CHRO from a well-known organization who is evaluating internal candidates for CEO succession. He began by explaining that the head of the CEO selection committee had asked him to develop the specs for the position. When I asked him whether the board was plugged into the organization's strategy, he told me that they were very much aware and involved in that strategy.

"Then why aren't they developing the specs with your assistance?"

He said that they wanted him "to get something on paper first."

I then inquired whether he had reviewed the specs he created with the incumbent CEO, and he admitted that the incumbent did indeed want to review the specs before he sent them on to the selection committee. He also added that the board committee intended to interview internal candidates en masse rather than in one-on-one sessions.

At first blush, this conversation may not seem overly disturbing, but it contains the seeds of numerous problems. Clearly, this CHRO is unable to stand up to his CEO and say that it's a bad idea for him to review the specs prior to the board committee's looking at them, that the CEO may be tempted to change them in a way that suits his personal agenda or reflects his biases. Just as alarming is the CHRO's willingness to write the specs on his own without any input from the board. Theoretically, the selection committee will have more combined strategic wisdom than the CHRO, and they should use it to do the first draft of the specs. Finally, this human resources chief needs to encourage board members to have one-on-one meetings with each candidate rather than try to save time through group interviews (which rarely produce the same insights about candidates as do one-on-one exchanges). If the CHRO maintains this passive role, it's likely that the internal search will become an external one sooner or later. The specs will be wrong and the interviews won't yield accurate information about candidates. Either the selection committee will identify dissatisfaction with their internal candidates and go outside, or they will hire the wrong internal person and may even be forced to do an external search later on.

CHROs who demonstrate leadership and a capacity of influence can often help their organizations avoid these mistakes. Because they have earned the respect of the CEO, the board, and other members of the executive team, they are proactive and talk straight when they see this selection process going off track. In fact, the CHRO's responsibility for making sure the company chooses the right CEO begins earlier than our other four players' roles. As the custodian of the company's development culture, the HR chief must keep the company well-stocked with talent and then grow it. When this is the case, the organization will find itself brimming with qualified candidates when it comes time to select the next CEO.

Here are five simple steps CHROs can take to enhance the internal selection process:

• *Put in place a dynamic system for recruiting, developing, identifying, and measuring high-potential people for promotion and possible CEO succession.* It's impossible to overemphasize the importance of this responsibility, as a recent McKinsey report attests. In a study of six thousand managers at seventy-seven companies, they determined that about 77 percent of corporate officers felt their companies had "insufficient talent sometimes" or were "chronically talent-short across the board." People often are under the mistaken notion that the search for a CEO successor starts a year or so before the incumbent leaves. In reality, the internal search starts many years earlier. Finding the right CEO today might be a result of recruiting a highly talented group of young executives twenty years ago.

CHROs need to focus on stocking their companies with talent long before they begin formal work on a succession plan. They must develop a system that attracts the best and the brightest and spotlights managers whose performance suggests that they might have what it takes to be CEO candidates. In addition, the CHRO must create performance metrics supported by the CEO and the board that avoid standardized or generic measures (or that reflect a CEO's biases) and are linked either to a business unit's or the company's strategy.

- *Update the board continuously about executive talent.* Though the incumbent CEO will probably work closely with the CHRO to monitor the performance and the promotability of high-potential people, the board also needs to be aware of what's happening with the talent in the organization. Ultimately, the CHRO is going to be called upon by the board to assist them in their CEO selection responsibilities. HR heads who have never bothered to inform the board about these issues will probably be viewed by the board as a mere functionary in the selection process. For this reason, CHROs should be empowered to establish an independent relationship with the appropriate board committee so the board knows that the CHRO is willing and able to provide assistance with any aspect of CEO succession. And an annual formal board meeting should be devoted to this task.

- *Encourage the board to conduct independent meetings to assess the performance of individual executives.* The board should not get all their information about internal candidates from the CEO. As I emphasized earlier, balance is what makes the process work, and the board can add balance if they have been able to meet and observe candidates over time and form their own opinions about them. A CHRO who encourages the board to meet this responsibility by arranging exposure to prospective candidates and providing updates on their performance will greatly facilitate the board's selection tasks.

- *Influence the board to begin succession planning at the appropri-ate time and the CEO to not take on any succession activity without the board's involvement.* These may seem like minor points, but they're actually quite significant. Board members sometimes take their eye off the ball; they can be tardy in starting the succession planning process. As a result, they scramble to find internal candidates or rush to select a candidate (and make a mistake because they rushed). Similarly, the CEO may ignore the board and take on suc-cession tasks by himself, thus depriving the process of the board's balancing input.

CHROs can't demand that the board get off their behinds and start planning, nor can they bully the CEO to stop monopolizing succession planning. They can, however, demonstrate capacity of influence. If they are respected by the board and CEO and viewed as a business partner, CHROs will often have sufficient influence that the board and CEO heed their suggestions regarding succession planning.

- *Work with the board committee to develop, monitor, and fine-tune CEO successor specs.* Perhaps the key term in the above sentence is *fine-tune.* I've already discussed the importance of getting the specs right, but here my point is that CHROs need to determine whether the specs are still right after time has passed and encourage the board to reformulate them if they are not. In an era of rapid change, CEO specs can easily evolve from the time the process is started to the time a CEO must be selected. HR chiefs simply need to make spec alteration an agenda item for the board to consider.

It takes courage to take these steps. In some instances, the CHRO may be putting his job on the line by challenging the CEO. Some chief executives may feel their HR heads are stepping over the line when they suggest that succession planning should com-mence in the near future. An insecure CEO, believing that a CHRO is intimating that he's over the hill, may respond, "You're going to start planning for retirement long before I will." Most CEOs, however, will see the light if a CHRO with a capacity of influence makes a well-reasoned argument along the following lines: "Your successor is now about twenty-five or thirty years of age, so we ought to be recruiting and observing young talent so that when you do plan to retire in fifteen years, we'll have developed our people to the point that you and the board will have at least a few highly qualified candidates to choose from."

External Insight

HR chiefs often play minor or purely administrative roles in external CEO searches. Search consultants would rather deal directly with boards and rely on CHROs for information only. The boards often have had little contact with HR executives in the past and don't view them as being part of the search team. The CEO may reinforce this perception. As mentioned previously, most board members have never participated in an external CEO search.

CHROs who are superb influencers, however, can lend crucial support and ideas to the search process. Let's examine the key contributions they can make:

• *Facilitate the board selection committee's work at the start of the process.* From servicing this committee to engaging them in discussions about developing the new CEO specs, CHROs can get the process off to a good start. They should monitor the timing of the search by helping the board determine when to start the process (twelve to fifteen months before the CEO's planned departure is usually about right). They can also make sure that the committee forms and begins work, providing them with information and ideas about how to develop the specs as well as making sure that the specs are linked to corporate strategy. This may entail retaining a strategy consultant who can help the board crystallize a strategic direction. If the board creates a spec document that is overly detailed or confusing, the CHRO—and a search consultant—can help reduce it to its essentials. If nothing else, he can encourage the board to achieve consensus about the specs that all candidates will be measured against.

• *Help select the search consulting firm and assist the chosen firm.*
Often CHROs are the most familiar with executive search consulting firms and in the best position to help the board choose an
appropriate one for a given search for positions below the CEO
level. But selecting a CEO search consultant is different, and the
CHRO must set aside past loyalties in favor of considering search
consultants with proven CEO search experience. CHROs often
complain that the selected CEO search consultant ignores them,
but they must realize that once a board takes on an external CEO
search and stops considering internal candidates, the search
becomes a board matter and is no longer the purview of the CHRO
or incumbent CEO. The search firm regards the board as their primary client.

However, CHROs can make significant contributions by
orchestrating search firm consultants' presentations to boards and
advising selection committees on what each firm will bring to the
search. Just as important, CHROs can provide invaluable assistance
to search consultants by serving as a conduit for information about
the organization's culture, compensation policies, and strategy. In
some cases, board members don't want to spend the time educating
the search consultant, or they don't have the answers the consultant needs. CHROs certainly shouldn't attempt to direct the search
or usurp the search consultant's responsibilities, but they can be
valuable allies in the often difficult process of finding the right candidate.

• *Add an objective and uniquely informed voice to the process.* A
CHRO is the one person other than the CEO who has a broad
exposure to the entire organization and doesn't have an ax to grind.
He may see things about the company and its future strategic
requirements that board members may overlook or miss. Even more
significant, if the CHRO has a strong relationship with the CEO,
he can offer the selection committee his sense of the incumbent's
leadership qualities and what made him an effective CEO for the
organization (assuming that he was effective). The CHRO's participation in the selection process also can reassure a CEO who may

otherwise feel shut out. If this CEO is comfortable in his skin, he will refrain from trying to use the CHRO to influence the search committee's decisions and trust his HR chief to make sure the process unfolds in a timely, informed, and efficient manner. I've also found that some CHROs give selection committees great questions to ask candidates and give candidates information about the company that the candidates otherwise might not have (and who might accept or reject an offer based on incomplete or wrong information).

There is one part of the process from which CHROs should be excluded: choosing the CEO. It's unfair to ask an HR chief to participate in the decision of who his next boss should be. By asking him to participate in a selection decision, the board may also be challenging his loyalty to his boss (who may not approve of any of the candidates or may wish to delay succession for another year or longer).

The Ideal Person for the Job, the Ideal Job for the Person

Not every CHRO will be a positive, balancing force in the selection process, and not every organization will provide the type of environment that enables a CHRO to be this force. But for the purposes of this chapter I'd like to ignore this reality and create a portrait of the ideal HR chief and the ideal organizational environment. My goal in doing so is to give individuals and organizations a target to shoot for, a target that if hit can add a fifth contributing player to the selection dynamic.

Ideally, CHROs will only take on this job in organizations where they're asked to be a member of the operating committee. Companies will recognize that the CHRO can be a business partner as well as an administrator, and they'll also structure the position so that the CHRO continuously interacts with the board and by serving the board's compensation committee and reporting to all board members about the state of leadership talent in the organization.

It's also important for CHROs to arrive at their jobs with the right combination of experiences. Again, the ideal would be for the young, upwardly mobile human resources executive to have spent time in finance, marketing, manufacturing, strategic planning, or corporate development and then move on to HR. Such experience would provide the broad business background that would enable this HR executive to contribute a business perspective rather than a purely HR perspective. If I were a CEO and wanted to "grow" the best possible CHRO, I would make sure he had the chance to be the head of HR for a business unit. The overly "staffy" HR people who have been stuck in corporate HR functions lack the business acumen to sit at the table with other top executives and board members.

From an individual standpoint, the ideal CHRO is a great lateral influencer, believes in straight talk, and is willing to level with the CEO, board members, and others. I've found that many HR executives consider themselves "people persons." As such, they are eager to please their bosses. They also tend to focus on people issues to the exclusion of all others. This may result in their being unable to pull the trigger on tough people decisions, such as firing, demoting, passing over for a promotion, and so on. In many instances, it also prevents them from providing the straight talk and business insights so crucial for a CHRO.

Finally, the ideal CHRO values his charge to keep the company well-stocked with executive talent. Almost to the point of obsession, this HR chief works hard to attract future leaders and monitors their performance for promotion. He views this responsibility as more important than making sure the company has access to the latest training materials or making sure policies are not being violated. Whenever I've interviewed a CHRO as part of a search assignment, I've asked him the following questions:

• How do you run your executive pipeline?
• How are you and the CEO involved in recruiting, developing, and measuring this talent?

- How do you get the board involved and keep them informed about the flow of leadership talent into the company and how these leaders are developing and progressing?

- How do you handle the inherent conflicts between what your CEO wants and what is in the best interests of your shareholders?

- What is your preferred method of working with search consultants?

- How will you help the new CEO assimilate into the organization?

CHROs who answer these questions with enthusiasm and knowledge are usually the ones who make the greatest contributions to the CEO selection process.

Chapter Nine

Problematic Scenarios

Situations and Events That Can Affect the CEO Selection Process

Ideally, the five players in the CEO selection dynamic will achieve the balanced participation described in the previous chapters. Realistically, they will find that certain situations or scenarios threaten this balance. Up to this point, I've described how dysfunctional CEOs, overly passive boards, and other factors can upset this balance. But as most of you know, there are countless scenarios that can throw the process off and result in a poor selection. Though I'm not going to address each and every scenario, I would like to focus on some of the more common situations that can have a significant effect on the selection process.

Specifically, I'd like to look at the following three broad categories of scenarios:

- *Time.* When companies feel pressure to replace a CEO quickly or spend egregiously long periods of time making up their minds, the process can be affected.

- *Environment.* Everything from being in a turnaround situation to the prospect of a merger to the need to maintain the momentum of a successful enterprise can play a major role in who is selected and how that selection is made.

- *People.* People situations arise that can skew the process and the decisions of the selection committee, including when a previous CEO successor selection has been fired or when an incumbent is extremely powerful and is excluding the board from selection decisions.

Let's look at each of these three categories with an eye toward how organizations can adjust so that a given scenario does not bias their judgment.

Rushing to Select or Moving like a Snail

I've known boards and incumbent CEOs who have made "instant" selections by spending little time developing thoughtful specifications or interviewing several candidates. At the other end of the spectrum, I've witnessed CEOs and boards who drag their heels and spend two or three years without arriving at a decision. The instant selection is especially problematic when you consider all the different reasons organizations rush to replace their CEOS:

- The organization waited too long to begin its search and the CEO's retirement date is fast approaching.
- The incumbent becomes ill or dies suddenly.
- The CEO successor is pirated away by another organization just before the final choice is made.
- The company is in trouble and needs new leadership fast.
- A great candidate becomes available and the company wants to grab him before another company does.
- An opportunity arises and the board believes it must put a new CEO in place to capitalize on it.

Although all these scenarios may make boards feel as if they need to choose a successor quickly, they should resist this impulse. In some instances, the time pressures are illusory; no real loss will be sustained by taking a few more months to do the selection right. In other instances, time is a legitimate factor, but even then a rush to replace the CEO can be avoided. In many instances, lead directors can assume the helm temporarily while the search is being conducted. When Compaq fired CEO Eckhard Pfeiffer, three board members took over the CEO role while the board went through the search process thoroughly and astutely and looking at both internal and external candidates (and eventually selecting an internal one).

High-speed searches have a frantic, panicky quality. In the rush to choose a successor, boards often give short shrift to position requirements and are too willing to compromise the specs. For example, they may begin the process by requiring candidates to possess proven international experience but then back off this requirement because they've found a candidate who meets other requirements. Or they may find someone who has only been moderately successful with acquisitions when being highly successful was the requirement, yet the company is willing to compromise because this candidate is the best one available and they don't want to take the time to search for others who might meet the spec. It's easy to rationalize these compromises due to the alleged need for speed, but organizations should never compromise the specs for this reason. When speed drives the specs, the result is usually a CEO who is a poor fit with an organization.

As I emphasized earlier, it usually takes between five and seven months to complete the search and selection process. Though much of this time is devoted to the actual tasks of selecting a CEO, some of it is necessary for contemplating the information gathered, as well as negotiating the complexities of the employment agreement. Creating the specs isn't something to be done off the top of your head. It takes some serious thinking before a board or incumbent CEO can distill the job requirements to five or six key traits. Our search for a new CEO for MassMutual started with twenty-seven candidate qualities before the board winnowed them down to seven essential "musts." Similarly, the selection committee should reflect on all the information they've learned about candidates; they need to spend some time by themselves and take a long, hard look at who best measures up to what the organization needs in a leader.

Speed is enticing, and it takes a strong search consultant, board, incumbent, CHRO, and candidate to resist the urge to rush. Boards, especially, are under pressure from the media to find a CEO successor relatively quickly. When companies have fired a CEO or when one has abruptly resigned, each day that passes without a choice can prove embarrassing to the board. As articles in trade publications speculate about possible candidates or as the *Wall Street Journal* reports on how long CEO searches take, board members become anxious. Boards or CEO incumbents may also want to move quickly because they fall in love with a superstar candidate. They learn that a top executive at General Electric or another high-profile company is available and decide that if they don't move quickly, they'll lose this star to the competition. But selecting a candidate based on his perceived star quality without a thorough analysis of the specs and accompanying selection process is a dangerous gambit. As well as an executive might have done elsewhere, there's no guarantee that he's going to repeat his success at another organization. In fact, his superstar status may be a result of his previous organization's resources or marketplace position as much as his own leadership skills.

Sometimes, of course, companies take too long to reach a decision. Whereas boards usually tend toward speed, controlling CEO incumbents tend to drag their feet. At times, CEOs aren't serious about finding their replacements. Consciously or not, they are conducting a search for show. I know one CEO who has been looking for two years for a successor and is now on his third search consulting firm; he complains that he just can't find the "right" person. More likely, he's reluctant to retire and the extended search is a stalling tactic. It's doubtful that any board members have questioned his intent. Searches like this that go on and on are like houses that remain on the market for months without selling; people assume there must be something wrong with them. Potential outside candidates are turned off when they're contacted by these companies; they assume that the companies must have big problems or someone would have been hired by now.

Obviously, some CEO searches are tougher than others and may require an additional few months above the norm. Though there's nothing wrong with taking some additional time to get it right, there is a problem when the amount of time becomes excessive or when a search is conducted primarily as a show of due diligence.

Save the Environment

Environment is a rather vague category, but it's a useful one in that issues can arise both within and outside an organization to throw the search off track. In essence, I'm defining *environment* to mean existing or emerging issues or cultures that are significant enough to catalyze dysfunctional behavior by one or more members of the search process. For instance, if a major competitor is making huge inroads through its e-commerce transformation, a board member may overreact and declare that their next CEO must have significant e-commerce experience. This may be an appropriate requirement, but it may also overwhelm the specs to the point that this board member (as well as others) is focused primarily on it. Or a CEO or board may declare that the problem is the top line when the real problem is the bottom line. As a result, a selection is made based on an emotional reaction to an environmental event rather than through considerable thought and deliberation.

The following are the types of environmental issues that can create problems in a CEO search and the recommended actions when faced with these environments:

- *Strongly imbedded institutional cultures.* In essence, the search committee is trying to find someone who can become a member of the "family" and keep the momentum going. Just like a father who doesn't think anyone is good enough for his daughter, the search committee may turn down qualified candidates because they have some small flaw. In other words, they start searching for the perfect CEO, a mythical figure. I recently counseled a new CEO that he had become head of a company with one of the most imbedded cultures in the world and that he needed to take it slow and not let the culture overwhelm him. These cultures are so powerful that they can destroy a placement even after the search has been successfully conducted and turn against the new CEO who finds himself unable to live up to the culture's written and unwritten attitudes and behaviors.

It's important, therefore, for the people involved in the search to acknowledge that their organization has a strongly imbedded institutional culture that poses certain challenges for outsiders. In fact, the search committee may want to discuss whether this culture is still viable, and if not, how it might change and who might be best able to change it. If the decision is made that the culture remains viable, then the search committee must discuss issues such as whether an internal candidate steeped in the culture might be better able to maintain and fit in with this culture than an external candidate. And if the committee does decide to look at external candidates, they should avoid falling into the perfection trap, recognize that maintaining the culture is only one of four or five key requirements, and judge candidates based on all these requirements. After all, even the best-run companies require transformation over time.

• *Turnaround situations.* When organizations are in trouble, it's generally much more difficult to attract the right external candidates (and sometimes, the right internal ones). Most top executives don't want to risk their future on a company that has two strikes against it. Turnarounds are tough, and the search process can sputter when the goal is to recruit a turnaround expert; there are just not that many of them out there. As a result, the search committee can pick someone who may seem to be a turnaround expert but in fact is a turnaround neophyte; he may have worked in an organization that had a dramatic about-face but wasn't directly responsible for it (or he might have been involved in one turnaround but that is the extent of his experience). People wish and pray so hard for someone to lead the company out of the wilderness that they can lose their objectivity when it comes to judging an individual's turnaround credentials.

If you're going to hire a turnaround expert, hire a *real* turnaround expert. There are executives who thrive on tough odds and live to reverse expectations and put companies back on their feet again. These situations require people who favor swift action and can pull the trigger quickly after looking at a minimum amount of data. These leaders possess a healthy narcissism, are risk takers, and have great confidence in the face of horrible odds. I've seen organizations hire turnaround neophytes who have taken too long to make decisions by analyzing when they should have been acting.

• *Big fish in a small pond.* At some point, a significant percentage of smaller companies decide they need to recruit a CEO from a larger corporation. They determine they must have a leader who has "heavyweight" experience and contacts. Perhaps they've had a string of "small" CEOs who have lacked the vision to move the company up to a new level. Everyone from dot-com start-ups to family-owned businesses have pursued CEOs working at Fortune 500 companies. Unfortunately, search committees can be blinded by the name of an organization and fail to see whether given executives fit their organization.

Too often, they don't. Typically, executives who have spent most of their working lives at large corporations are accustomed to having others execute their orders. They also have grown to rely on access to large amounts of financial data for decision making and are used to moving carefully and slowly. Some of them are "Peter Principled" or stalled in place, whereas others feel stuck at a certain level in their large organizations and think it would be more challenging to be the CEO of a smaller one. Although some executives can handle the large-to-small transition, many cannot. They find the roll-up-your-sleeves mentality and the need to become more personally involved with customers and staff off-putting. Others cannot cope with the ambiguities and resist pulling the trigger quickly on important decisions.

Therefore, be careful about making big company experience the number one selection criteria for a smaller company. Instead, focus on the fit between a potential candidate's personality and track record and the company's strategic needs rather than the prestige or size of the company with which he was involved.

- *Recruiting from a competitor.* A number of years ago, Volkswagen successfully recruited GM purchasing star Jose Ignacio Lopez de Arriotua amid allegations by GM that their former purchasing executive stole proprietary information. Since then, there have been numerous cases in which CEOs recruited from competitors have stirred up bad feelings and lawsuits, with the result that the selected candidates have reneged when the heat became too intense.

Although there certainly are instances when companies may want to target competitors, they need to exercise a degree of caution and common sense. Imagine spending months defining the specs, identifying and interviewing candidates, and finally selecting an individual who eventually withdraws or is forced out because of all the competitive hullabaloo surrounding the recruiting effort.

Here are some simple rules that will help companies recruit CEO candidates from competitors fairly and with the most likelihood of keeping the selection process moving forward:

Before interviewing a potential candidate, clearly communicate that the purpose of the interview is to explore potential employment and not industry-competitive matters. Verify that he has not signed a noncompete agreement.

If a candidate offers competitive information voluntarily during the interview process, beware! He may well feel equally free to dispense confidential information about his new company.

Don't hire other top executives from the same company for at least a year to avoid even the appearance of impropriety.

- *Mergers and acquisitions.* These major events can throw off succession plans and create internecine battles between CEOs. Any company attempting to select a CEO either as a mandate or prior to a merger should confirm that candidates understand that their position may be tenuous if a larger or more powerful entity materializes as the dominant partner. Heavyweight negotiations should occur prior to the merger that define who will be the chairman, what the "old" CEO's role will be, how the succession pipeline will be reshaped, and who the key players will be going forward.

Boards must take responsibility for defining these issues beforehand, as well as disclosing merger or acquisition possibilities. When the search is for the CEO of two later-to-be-merged entities, the search committee needs to communicate the reasons for the merger and the issues—both negative and positive—now facing the prospective new company. It's a major mistake to hide negative facts such as the desperate straits that drove the two companies into each other's arms or the political in-fighting that has occurred since the merger. Candidates and their suitors are much better off when the latter can decide with full knowledge whether they want to lead a "reborn" company that is undergoing growing pains.

• *Political divisions.* Personal or cultural biases can play havoc with the selection process. In companies with functional silos—where marketing and engineering don't talk, for instance—the choice of a successor can be influenced by which function has the most power. In some instances, people from certain functions are excluded from succession because they come from "weak" groups. In other situations, a CEO who "grew up" in one function wants his successor to come from that same function, whether or not he's the best qualified candidate.

Boards, too, can be split into factions that favor certain types of candidates. Often factions are related to evaluating a candidate's experience improperly. One board member doesn't even want to consider anyone who lacks extensive experience in the company's industry, whereas another director may want a broader background. Sometimes personal bias divides board members, biases related to age, gender, ethnicity, appearance, compensation, and even marital status.

To a certain extent, healthy disagreement and debate among board members is a positive sign. Someone, however, has to bring the discussion back to the specs and point out the disconnects (often the search consultant, if it's an external search). Rather than engaging in endless debate about subjective selection issues, the search committee must refocus their discussion on the real job requirements. Decision makers must get past their personal opinions and feelings about what type of person should be CEO and arrive at a consensus on who is the best fit for what the organization needs based on its strategic goals, culture, and other related factors.

The People Puzzle

The personalities and predilections of individuals often create scenarios that can thwart the best of intentions. Everyone from legacy-driven CEOs to overly demanding candidates can unbalance the process and produce a less-than-ideal CEO selection. I've talked quite a bit about certain people issues such as the overly egotistical CEO and the rubber stamp board (that will do everything a powerful CEO wants), and I don't want to go over that territory again. But there are other people issues that create confusing scenarios, and these are the ones I'd like to address here:

- *The CEO who drives successors away.* Although driving candidates away may not be the conscious intent, it is the effect. Some legacy CEOs such as Armand Hammer at Occidental and Bill Paley at CBS stayed in office so long that successors became impatient and left, assuming that their boss was never going to depart. (Gerry Roche recruited three CEOs to CBS before one stuck!) Other CEOs make a great show of choosing their successors or conducting an external search but deep down don't really want to leave. As I've recounted, many retired CEOs retain a significant amount of power in their organizations, and their looming presence (on the board, in the building, or both) makes it difficult for the new CEO to blaze his own trail. Some newly appointed CEOs may believe they have carte blanche; for the first year or so, that might be true. Sometimes, however, all it takes is a failed project or a drop in market share for the old, sleeping CEO to wake and roar, "Enough!" I've also seen CEO successors incur the wrath of the incumbent by doing minor things such as shuttering the executive dining room, bumping the about-to-retire incumbent off the company plane so he could use it, or granting an interview to a publication that does a flattering profile of the successor and takes a swipe at the outgoing CEO. In some of these situations, the CEO-successor was forced out by the incumbent, who either remained on the board or kept meddling in company affairs through his relationships with board cronies.

In all these scenarios, the board should step up and make sure that the transition goes smoothly. If a succession plan had been put in place, they should continuously monitor its implementation and speak up if things don't go according to plan. If they've selected a new CEO, they should stand by their choice. Admittedly, this is difficult to accomplish when the incumbent or retired CEO is powerful; it's also a problem if he remains on the board or in the building. But if boards recognize that a CEO is sabotaging their or his own successor choices because he fears retirement, they need to make their stand for the good of the company and the sake of their shareholders.

- *The fired CEO effect.* In some circumstances, search committees and search consultants are looking to replace a CEO fired by the board. Certainly this can place the company in a difficult position, in that candidates will naturally wonder, If it happened to him, might it happen to me? For this reason, the search committee must be up-front with candidates about why the previous CEO was fired and make a good case for why it was justified. These searches can also be difficult because the company may be in trouble—a good reason for firing the CEO if he was responsible for the trouble —and finding someone able and willing to lead a troubled company can be challenging.

I've found, however, that the reason behind the firing can be the basis for a bull's-eye spec. Let's say the previous CEO was fired because he verbally brutalized his people and dropped morale as far as it could go. As a result, the company experienced a talent drain as key executives departed. The new spec, therefore, might revolve around someone who is proven to be both a strong personality and good at followership; who is skilled at relating to people and can attract, develop, and motivate executive talent. Rather than ignoring the reasons the former CEO was fired, search committees should discuss them at length and develop specs around them.

• *The CEO runs the search by himself.* No matter what the corporate bylaws say, the CEO feels he's entitled to hand-pick his successor, whether from inside or outside. Though he may involve the board, the CHRO, and the search consultant, he doesn't include them in the decision-making process. They have no real say in who is selected. Early in my career, I was working with an incumbent CEO on a search for his successor and I asked him about involving the board in the process. He replied, "They'll have dinner with the person I select." He was dysfunctional, and I didn't realize it.

I didn't know any better back then, but boards, search consultants, and CHROs should know better today. In fact, the CHRO of the aforementioned company was a highly talented executive who recognized that the organization would be in trouble if this CEO was allowed to control the search. The CHRO had established a good relationship with the chairman of the board's compensation committee, and together they helped the board become more involved in the process. Ultimately, the board approved the selection of a CEO candidate who the incumbent slightly disagreed with but who was a good fit for the organization's future strategic requirements. A postscript: To their credit, the board resisted the retiring CEO's attempts to unseat his successor after a year, and the new CEO has enjoyed a successful run now for many years.

• *Internal succession is a mess.* A confused or convoluted succession plan (or lack thereof) brings out the worst in people. I've talked about how internal competitions or "horse races" can cause candidates to act in unnatural and unproductive ways as they attempt to please the CEO-kingmaker, but the lack of a good succession plan can create political infighting and divisiveness among candidates, board members, and others. In some companies, the situation is further exacerbated by a series of prestigious executive titles that give the impression to more than one executive that they're next in line for the CEO job. These titles—executive vice president, vice chairman, chief operating officer—often convey a false sense of who the candidates are and their pecking order. The result: Machiavellian scheming, bruised egos, and an unnecessary loss of talent.

Succession plans need to be created earlier, clearly detailed, shared with the board, and updated as the situation demands. Responsibilities should clearly communicate where each executive stands and not give a false impression about who is a candidate. Succession planning is serious business, and if the CEO, CHRO, and the board take it that way, it won't give rise to the infighting that can hamper the CEO selection process.

The Keys to Handling Problematic Scenarios Effectively

In most of the scenarios discussed, the key players made mistakes when panic, bias, and politics were allowed to play major roles in the CEO selection process. It doesn't take much more than a board responding to media pressure to make a quick selection for the wrong CEO to be picked. A board seeking the mythical perfect candidate can doom a search. A powerful CEO may not realize how his power is preventing the right successor from being selected.

When faced with a problematic scenario, organizations must resolve to handle it objectively, calmly, and with reasonable speed. In most instances, boards have more time than they think to select a CEO. In most situations, the selection committee is composed of people with great intelligence and perception who can make a selection without being unduly influenced by a recent merger or a previously bungled CEO selection.

If all those involved in the succession and selection processes take a deep breath, resolve to work together in a balanced, objective manner, and move forward with diligence but not haste, they can handle most problematic scenarios that come their way.

Chapter Ten

Benchmarking the CEO Selection Process

Is your organization prepared to select a new CEO? Is your succession planning process in good shape? More specifically, will your company's CEO insist on remaining on the board after his successor assumes office? Will your board members work diligently, perceptively, and objectively to select the right CEO for your organization?

These are tough questions that must be answered thoughtfully and thoroughly. If they're left hanging or if your company is content with vague answers, you run a real risk of selecting the wrong person for the job. This chapter is designed to help you arrive at useful answers. By the end of it, you should have a sense of whether your CEO selection process is capable of identifying the candidates who will best be able to lead your organization in the years to come.

To a certain extent, your analysis will be colored by your position within the organization (or outside it). If you're the CEO of a company, you're likely to view the following benchmarking tools differently than if you're a CHRO. Perspectives on a given company's CEO selection strengths and weaknesses are colored by individual roles. When you put your role under the microscope, you may find this view makes it difficult to remain completely objective. Objectivity, however, is crucial. As difficult as it might be for a director to admit that the board is overly influenced by a powerful CEO's preferences or for a CHRO to recognize that he is not viewed as an equal by other members of the management team, such recognitions are key. The more unbiased you are in your benchmarking, the more likely the result will lead to increased efficacy in CEO succession and selection.

Analysis of Checks and Balances

The interrelationships among board members, the incumbent CEO, the search consultant, the CHRO, and the CEO candidates are multifaceted and problematic. In the mix are powerful egos, psychological issues, and friendships. The CEO selection process functions best when a system of checks and balances is established and when these five participants operate in an environment of creative tension, where open dialogue and debate are the norms. No one person dominates the process and no easy assumptions about who should be CEO are left unchallenged.

Do the relationships among the five players in your selection dynamic reflect this balance? The checklists in Table 10.1 describe a balanced dynamic and an unbalanced one. Which one best describes your organization?

Straight-Talk Audit

You may suspect that your CEO selection process will be unbalanced, but you're not quite sure where the problem lies. It may be that board members more than any of the other participants are upsetting the dynamic. Or it may be that two or three of the participants are the source of problems. Straight talk—or the lack thereof—is a great way to identify who is contributing to an effective process and who is not. As you review the statements in Table 10.2, determine who in your organization is capable of this type of straight talk and who is incapable of making these statements (and meaning them).

Scenarios

The following are common situations in selecting a CEO where the process can take one of two directions. After the description of these situations, you'll find a wrong response (Response A) and a

Table 10.1. Checklist for Balance in the CEO Selection Process

Balanced	Unbalanced
___ The CEO views board members as equals and welcomes their questions and criticism.	___ The CEO treats board members like employees and expects them to do his bidding.
___ Board members take their governance responsibilities seriously, are attentive at board meetings, and are well informed about the company's strategy.	___ Board members rarely challenge the CEO's actions and decisions.
___ The CHRO reports to the CEO, meets independently with the board, and is considered an equal member of the management team.	___ CEO search consultants are "handled" by the CHRO and have little or no board contact.
___ The CHRO and the CEO have institutionalized procedures for identifying and developing internal candidates as part of the succession process.	___ Everyone knows that the CEO's retirement is a sham and that he will establish a scenario to still be in control after his official retirement.
___ The CEO makes sure the board is regularly briefed about the succession process.	___ The internal candidate with the inside track on the CEO job naively believes that his appointment to COO will automatically and quickly lead to becoming the CEO.
___ Potential internal CEO candidates frequently make presentations to the board.	___ Board members focus much of their energy and attention on the social aspects of being on the board.
___ Search consultants are viewed as partners in the search process and are not asked to "fetch" candidates or complete the search in a few weeks.	___ Everyone knows that an external search will be undertaken but that it's largely an empty exercise because the successor has already been covertly selected.

Table 10.2. Straight-Talk Audit

Board Member	Incumbent CEO	Candidate
___ We (the board) have created a contingency plan in case our CEO decides to leave suddenly, is fired, or dies.	___ I have discussed my retirement with the board of directors and set a definite date for that retirement.	___ I will not naively believe everything that the CEO incumbent tells me.
___ I am cognizant of the major challenges that will face a new CEO.	___ I will not remain on the board of directors after I retire.	___ I will not be so eager to become CEO that I will accept without a written agreement.
___ We will meet at least twice each year to discuss strategic planning as well as to review executive manpower.	___ I will not keep an office at company headquarters.	___ I will meet independently with each board member before accepting a job.
___ I insist on conducting serious, in-depth interviews with more than one CEO candidate.	___ The board and I have agreed on a succession timetable.	___ I will not participate in an internal horse race for the CEO spot.
___ We will not start a search before we've agreed on the CEO specifications.	___ Even if the board selects a candidate who isn't my first choice, I will not attempt to veto their selection.	___ I intend to rely not on company insiders to tell me about the organization but also to ask questions of the search consultant so I am fully informed before making a decision.
___ We began the process of identifying and testing internal CEO candidates at least five years before our CEO was scheduled to retire.	___ I believe every board member should interview my successor.	
___ I consider selection of a new CEO a critical responsibility and will be objective and diligent in an effort to find the right candidate under a realistic time frame.	___ I will delegate the engagement of a CEO search consultant to my board.	___ As much as I might want a given CEO position, I won't throw my hat in the ring if the incumbent CEO and the CHRO are the *only* ones controlling the search.
	___ I will discuss date-certain succession issues with prospective candidates and won't mislead them about my postretirement role.	

Table 10.2. Straight-Talk Audit *(Continued)*

CEO Search Consultant	CHRO
___ I will not accept a search assignment if the board and the incumbent CEO are at odds about the specs.	___ I do not view my role in the selection process as being a hench-man for the incumbent CEO.
___ I will not accept a search assignment if the board clearly isn't well informed about the strategic issues facing the company.	___ I am a member of the company operating (or management) committee and attend all sessions.
___ I will not accept a search assignment if the board wants me to pull an existing slate of candidates out of my hat *quickly.*	___ I will do everything possible to ensure that our board has direct exposure to all internal potential CEO candidates.
___ I will do whatever research and interviewing is necessary to develop a list of potential candidates whose qualifications are tailored to the position specs.	___ I meet independently with the board.
___ I will protect the confidentiality of the search unless the client directs me otherwise.	___ I do not feel that I should control the CEO search consultant.
___ I intend to talk to each board member before beginning the search.	___ I will stand up to the CEO if I feel he is attempting to apply undue influence on me or the board in the selection of the next CEO.
___ Even after a candidate is selected, I will continue to be involved in the process during the negotiation stage and be available to the board, the incumbent CEO, and the new CEO after terms have been agreed upon, including a candidate follow-up within the first year.	

right response (Response B) to the situations. You may well have already encountered these types of situations in the real world and made the correct choice. The issue here, however, is not your choice but the likely response of your organization. Decide what your company would probably do if it were confronted with these scenarios.

Turnaround Troubles

Mammoth Corporation was in trouble. It had endured five straight quarters of significant losses after years of being in the black. Though the biggest problem was low-priced foreign competitors, it was also suffering from a recycled strategy that was no longer viable given the current market conditions. Bill, the CEO for the past five years, had been ill for the last ten months. At first, it was thought that he would recover quickly, but the illness has dragged on and he has announced his retirement.

Vincent, the chairman of the board's search committee, convened the committee to discuss the problems they were facing. He explained that they needed to take action quickly, they were under increasing pressure from the financial community to turn things around, and that "all of us [board members] have our reputations on the line." Vincent told the committee that they could go about the search in the traditional manner and bring in a search consultant who would help orchestrate a process that could take six months or longer.

What Vincent recommended, however, was taking advantage of a relationship he enjoyed with Robert, the well-known former CEO of a major retailer. Robert made his reputation years ago with two stunning turnarounds of retailers in trouble. Though Robert hadn't done much in recent years—in fact, he had stumbled a bit when he was called upon to reverse the fortunes of other companies—he still enjoyed a superstar reputation. Charismatic, handsome, and a highly paid speaker on the business lecture circuit, Robert had been itching to get his hands on another company. Even though Mammoth Corporation was not in the retailing business, they did need someone who could work some magic. Vincent recommended they act now before another company made Robert an offer. He suggested they hire a search consultant to go through the motions of a formal search but that they prepare a deal with Robert and agree to go with him if no other candidates are identified.

Response A

My organization would probably agree with Vincent's suggestion and hire Robert. We are highly sensitive to any criticism from the financial community, and if we had five straight losing quarters we probably could rationalize choosing speed over due diligence. It would be different if we had developed internal people as CEO candidates, but our succession planning has been largely nonexistent. The lure of a superstar CEO would be too much for us to resist if we were in a turnaround situation.

Response B

We would never go along with Vincent's suggestion. Our board members take their responsibilities seriously and would never take this type of shortcut or be seduced by a CEO's star power. If we were in dire straits such as the one described, we would bring in a search consultant and work with him to figure out what the specs for the job really are. Essentially, we'd analyze what sort of person is best qualified to turn around our organization. We would define four or five very specific traits and then look for the candidate who has them. We would take the time to do things right. If our current CEO was too ill to carry out his duties, one of our board members could take over temporarily while the search was in progress. It's also possible that we would find the right candidate internally because we have an excellent succession plan and our board is well aware of who the potential candidates are.

THE POWERFUL CEO

Donna has been the CEO of Zenon Corporation for fifteen years, and she has turned it from a sleepy midsized company to an industry leader. During that period, she has appointed her people to the company's top positions and brought in the majority of board members. Donna is a traditional command-and-control leader who enjoys great respect on Wall Street as well as within the organization.

A few years ago, Donna reached the company's mandatory retirement age but was able to convince the board to extend her tenure on the grounds that they had no suitable internal successor. Though there was a succession plan in place, Donna was dissatisfied with the performance of all the people being groomed as potential CEO candidates. Still, she agreed to retire after her sixty-eighth birthday and stayed on the sidelines as the board engaged a search consultant and eventually selected a candidate.

During the negotiations with this candidate, however, Donna suggested to the board that she remain as nonexecutive chairwoman for an indefinite period to help the new CEO with the transition. Donna made a persuasive case to the board, emphasizing her great relationship with financial analysts as well as her knowledge about the organization and its strategy. Eventually, the board agreed to her suggestion and Donna not only was named chairwoman but was allowed to retain her office. The new CEO, who was tremendously impressed with Donna's accomplishments over the years, agreed to go along with the arrangement after Donna reassured him that she considered him the boss and herself a "resource" that he could draw upon.

After a few months, however, Donna proved to be more than a resource. She second-guessed the new CEO's decisions at every turn and took up a great deal of his time by barging into his office and lecturing him about "the way things are done around here." Soon, a number of senior executives were bringing issues and ideas to Donna rather than to the new CEO. Despite all this, the new chief executive was doing a good job and had made a number of strategic moves that were already bearing fruit. But by the end of the year, he was fed up with Donna's interference and expressed his ire at a board meeting. Essentially, he told the board that they had to get rid of Donna if they wanted him to remain as CEO.

Response A

We would try to convince the new CEO to live with Donna for a bit longer. Our incumbent CEO is similarly powerful, and it's likely that he too would be reluctant to relinquish his power. In fact, he already has an arrangement with the board to keep his office and will serve on the board after he retires. Many of our board members are beholden to our CEO; he has not only appointed board members but contributed to their charities and helped their friends get jobs. There's a social bond between our CEO and the board members that would be hard to break. Even if the Zenon board members believe the new CEO is doing a solid job, they're likely to side with Donna because their relationship with her trumps their responsibility to the company. It is probable that our board members would feel the same way if placed in a similar situation.

Response B

As much as we respect our CEO and as successful as he has been, we would never tolerate Donna's manipulative behaviors and allow her to exert her influence after the new CEO takes over. In fact, our CEO has signed off with the board on a very detailed succession plan that includes his agreement to leave the company and the premises after he officially retires. While he'll be available to the new CEO during a one-year transition period, he will be off-site and be brought in only at the new CEO's discretion. In addition, our CEO has encouraged both the board and the CHRO to point out to him when he's overstepping his authority with regard to the CEO succession process. He admitted that there may be times when he becomes "overly enthusiastic" about helping the company find his successor, and if he crosses any lines, he wants to be told to "back off." His retirement is still a few years off, but we've already identified and are observing a few solid internal candidates if we decide not to look outside for a successor.

THE FLEXIBLE SEARCH CONSULTANT

Carl worked for one of the world's largest executive search consulting firms. He was brought in by Wilmatta Corporation, a Fortune 100 company, to conduct a search for a new CEO. Carl was contacted by the CHRO and given the general parameters of the search. He also talked briefly with the CEO, who told him that the CHRO would be his main contact and that there was no reason to meet with the board until it came time to present candidates. The CEO also instructed him to include a vice president at another organization on his list of candidates, assuring Carl that "he's one of the best-qualified candidates you've ever encountered."

At first, Carl struggled with what he should do. He complained to the CHRO that he didn't have a particularly good sense of what the specs were and that he thought it might be

smart to meet with some board members who could illuminate the requirements of the CEO position. The CHRO suggested instead that he run interference for Carl and deal with
the board, since "they can be difficult at times." A week later,
the CHRO presented Carl with a list of CEO job requirements that were so general that they were almost useless.

Carl was tempted to resign from the search, suspecting
that it was a sham and that the CEO would appoint his
hand-picked candidate regardless of who Carl identified as
candidates. At the same time, Carl was under pressure to
increase his billings, and this assignment was a lucrative
piece of cake. Rationalizing that the CEO of Wilmatta would
just hire a competitor for the assignment if he bowed out,
Carl reluctantly went ahead with the search.

Response A

I suspect that our CEO has a hand-picked candidate who he's
going to make sure becomes his successor, no matter who a
search turns up. Though the scenario may not play out exactly
as it did at Wilmatta, the end result will be that our board has
little input about succession and will end up putting on a "due
diligence" show for stockholders and the media. By and large,
our board is accustomed to following our CEO's lead in all
matters; he has them well-trained. Our CHRO, too, would
never stand up to the CEO and tell him that he doesn't think
a sham search is in the best interests of the organization. I can
easily see our CHRO controlling a search consultant and
keeping him away from our board during the process.

Response B

This would be an unlikely scenario at our organization
because our board has a history of being involved in the
succession planning process and is well-versed in the business
issues facing the company. Even if our CEO and CHRO

conspired to keep them out of the process, they wouldn't stand for it. In fact, most of the current board was there seven years ago when we conducted an outside search for a CEO, and they worked closely with a search consultant who helped identify a strong slate of candidates, one of whom became the current CEO. This isn't to say that no tension would exist between the CEO and the board in terms of who ultimately would be selected. Our CEO has a strong personality and has a few internal people he's keen on developing as potential successors. Still, he and the board enjoy a healthy relationship with a lot of give and take. Neither our CEO nor the board (nor the CHRO, for that matter) would condone a search that was just an exercise rather than a real effort to find the best candidate.

Reflecting on Tough Choices

The following multiple-choice questionnaire is created not as a test but as an opportunity to reflect on the often confusing decisions that come with the territory. From the moment succession planning begins until a compensation package is negotiated, a series of vexing choices present themselves. You'll find these same vexing choices reproduced here. The goal isn't to make the correct choice—I'm assuming most of you know what that is—but to reflect on what your organization might do when these choices have to be made. What sorts of discussions might take place among board members? How will the decisions be made and who will make them? Who is likely to throw up a roadblock in front of the right decisions?

These are all questions to contemplate as you consider the multiple choices.

1. Your company has an internal CEO successor who has long been considered the front-runner, and the incumbent has made him an informal promise that he's going to get the job if he

hangs in there. But between then and now, the organization's strategy has changed and it's clear that the company needs a leader with skills different from ones he possesses. What would your organization do?

a. Give him the job because he deserves it.

b. Appoint him COO for a trial period and see how he does.

c. Tell him he'll be the front-runner if the search doesn't result in a candidate.

d. Hire a search consultant to identify candidates whose skills best match the organization's requirements.

2. You've winnowed the list of CEO candidates down to two external choices. One candidate is a vice president with one of the most well-known and respected companies in the world whereas the other is a COO of a much less well-known company. The former is considered a prize catch but the latter's expertise and experience are an excellent fit with the specs. What would your organization do?

a. Choose the latter candidate because of the match with the specs.

b. Choose the former candidate because of the positive publicity.

c. Look for a compromise candidate who has a higher profile than the latter but isn't quite as good a match with the specs.

d. Hire both candidates and let them fight it out for the top spot.

3. Amid a great deal of public criticism and controversy, your board has fired the CEO and is looking for his replacement. To that end, the board is interviewing search consultants and finds one who immediately presents them with a list of candidates who have sterling credentials and who the search consultant guarantees would be interested in the position. What would your organization do?

a. Immediately hire this consultant because he obviously knows the top candidates in the field.

    b. Look for another search consultant who can guarantee a quick turnaround, since speed is critical.

    c. Look for another search consultant who has a CEO-search track record of finding the right candidate by taking the time and putting in the effort to get it right.

    d. Avoid search consultants entirely in the interest of saving time and money and handle the search in-house.

4. After selecting a CEO candidate, the board begins experiencing doubts about their selection because the candidate is making his acceptance of the job contingent upon two actions: getting the incumbent CEO's retirement date in writing and being allowed to talk one-on-one with board members. What would your organization do?

    a. Withdraw the offer because this candidate is making unrealistic demands and isn't properly grateful just to be offered the job.

    b. Withdraw the offer because this candidate might turn the job down if he's allowed to question board members about the company and discovers some of its weaknesses.

    c. Agree to the conditions because they're reasonable.

    d. Make a counteroffer of permitting the candidate to talk to a designated group of board members and agreeing only to a verbal promise of a date-certain retirement.

5. You have three superbly qualified internal CEO candidates and don't want to lose the two who aren't selected. To avoid this possibility, what would your organization do?

    a. Select the best-qualified candidate and take the risk of losing the other two candidates.

    b. Declare each executive a candidate and communicate that their performance over the next six months will determine who wins the CEO job.

    c. Find an external candidate in order to avoid choosing one of the internal candidates over the other two.

    d. Name one as CEO, the second as COO, and the third as vice chairman so that everyone feels he has been rewarded.

Answers

1. a. The search must focus on identifying the best-qualified candidate for the job now and in the future. Too often, boards and incumbent CEOs view the CEO position as a reward for years of loyal service. Too often, they become accustomed to thinking of a particular executive as the heir apparent. In these instances, it may feel disloyal to tell a favorite son that he no longer is the best candidate for the job. But it's the right thing to do, not only for the organization but for the individual in question (because he'll probably fail at a job he's not qualified for).

2. a. The specs are what count! As tempting as it might be to choose the high-profile candidate, it usually turns out to be a mistake if he isn't the one whose talents best match the specs. When you find a candidate who is a good match with the specs, it makes no sense to look for a compromise candidate who might have a higher profile.

3. b. The tough choice here is between the possibility of a long and uncertain search process versus the appearance of a quick fix. This is an especially tough choice when a company feels pressure to replace a CEO quickly. Don't give in to that pressure. Organizations greatly increase the odds of making the right choice by hiring a search consultant who does his homework and takes the time to find truly qualified candidates for one specific organization. The easiest thing for any search consultant to do is to provide a shopping list of attractive candidates.

4. c. This a tough decision if the board knows it's going to cause friction with the incumbent CEO to get him to agree in writing to a retirement date. It's also tough if the board feels it has something to hide about the company and worries that one-on-one conversations with board members will expose a weakness or their lack of knowledge about corporate strategy. But these are two reasonable contingencies, and the process is

better served when date-certain retirement and conversations with board members are part of the deal.

5. a. It's not easy for a board to make a decision that might deprive the company of executive talent, but it's a chance worth taking if the best candidate for the company gets the job; the right choice will more than make up for the loss of two talented executives. The other alternatives—staging a horse race, avoiding making the choice altogether—won't guarantee that you'll keep all three executives and may also result in a poor selection.

Analyzing the Results

Although no definitive score can be obtained from this benchmarking exercise, you should be able to get a very good sense of how your organization will perform when it comes to selecting a new CEO. The key to reading the results of your benchmarking is to look for recurring themes. Reflect on what types of responses keep surfacing and which participant (or participants) in the process seem likely to unbalance it.

If, for instance, you decided that your company would choose the "wrong" responses to the posed scenarios, was there a common culprit for those wrong responses? Was it the same culprit who was identified in the straight-talk audit?

Even if you can't identify a single likely cause of a future process breakdown, this chapter will help your organization by stimulating the type of straight talk that is needed about these important issues. As speculative as some of these benchmarking activities are and as subjective as your responses might be, they will combine to yield rich discussions about your organization's capacity to make the right decision in selecting a CEO.

Chapter Eleven

Evolution of CEO Selection

The Best Direction

It would be nice to think that we've learned from our mistakes and will do a better job of selecting CEOs in the future. Ideally, CEOs, boards, and others involved in the selection process will learn to engage in straight talk and find the right CEO for their organizations. Given GE's tremendous results, more companies will probably adopt GE's succession model in order to achieve CEO bench strength.

Though it's impossible to know whether all these things will come to pass, they should be the focus of debate and discussion among board members and their CEOs. In fact, all five players in the CEO selection dynamic should devote more time and attention to what they can do to increase the dynamic's efficacy. Selecting a CEO has become not only a more important task than ever before but also a more challenging one. The complex issues confronting us today demand CEOs who are well matched in skills and temperament to the organizations they lead. At the same time, finding these CEOs may well take more time, energy, and perspicacity than in the past; companies have increasingly specific strategic requirements that can't be met by just any candidate with an impressive list of accomplishments.

In this final chapter, I'd like to look ahead and speculate where we might be going based on where we've been. It's a good news–bad news forecast, and I'd like to begin with two of the bad trends that show no signs of abating.

Subordinating CEO Succession Planning

Recently, the CEO of a $5 billion manufacturing company acknowledged the importance of developing executive talent internally but also admitted that he was unwilling to devote the resources necessary to develop this talent. As he said, "It is too expensive."

As organizations become more focused on short-term financial goals and cost containment, programs designed to develop executive talent seem increasingly vulnerable. If this trend continues, more companies will have to go outside to find their next CEO. When companies go outside, they're more likely to make a poor selection than if they've systematically developed internal people to take over the top job.

It's astonishing that any enlightened organization would neglect this fundamental task at a time when CEO tenure is shorter than ever before and the challenges facing each organization require a well-chosen leader. Nonetheless, companies often are burdened with neglected or poorly conceived succession plans and the lack of a well-funded program designed to recruit, retain, and develop executive talent. Perhaps this trend is due in part to CEOs who sincerely believe they will keep their jobs longer than they actually will. Perhaps it stems from the belief that search consultants can find a great CEO with relative ease and speed. Perhaps it's simply a result of an environment where most long-term programs are relegated to secondary importance.

Whatever the reason, this neglect handicaps an organization as it searches for a successor by denying the board an internal option. The lack of this option presents a number of problems. First, it means companies can't measure external candidates against internal ones. Second, the company will select a CEO who, no matter how talented or experienced, will still have a learning curve to climb. Unlike an internal candidate, the external selection needs to spend some time learning the company's culture and strategy, thus making it difficult for him to hit the ground running.

Think about all the praise GE has received for the way they selected a new CEO and quickly replaced the two CEO successors who left the company after the decision was made. The media reported the story as though GE had pulled off a miracle. In fact, they did what was normal and expected: They put a succession plan in place and made sure it was implemented properly. It took less than two weeks! In this day and age, however, such an action is considered unusual. That fact says a lot about where companies are falling down on the job.

The Quick and Easy Mentality

One of the themes I've stressed throughout this book is embodied in Mr. Rogers's phrase "Isn't it nice to have the time to do things right!" Unfortunately, we often *feel* as though we don't have that luxury in a world where deadlines are tighter and workloads are heavier. It's unusual if a board and its CEO aren't periodically confronted with a crisis. Typically, CEOs and boards feel tremendous competitive pressures because of new global competition, emerging technologies, mergers and acquisitions that reshape the marketplace, and e-commerce trends. It's not just boards and CEOs but all the people involved in the selection process who feel the pressure to make decisions quickly; it's human nature to look for shortcuts in this environment.

For these reasons, selection teams sometimes compress the process to the point that a poor choice is made. Years ago, most companies took their time before selecting a new CEO. They went about the task with great seriousness, and everyone involved in the selection did their homework. Although it was admittedly easier to select a CEO years ago (for no other reason than the job was easier), the right people were generally selected because a sufficient number of appropriate candidates were thoroughly researched and interviewed, the specs were well defined from the beginning, and the candidate who fit the specs usually got the job.

Today, selection committees gravitate toward shortcuts, including these:

- Search consultants provide boards with a recycled list of CEO candidate names.
- Boards or incumbent CEOs recruit a star for the position and ignore or downplay the specs.
- Boards rubber-stamp an incumbent CEO's "favorite son" candidate.
- Search committees interview only one or two candidates.
- Companies skip the crucial step of getting the specs right and start interviewing candidates right away.

There are no shortcuts when it comes to selecting a CEO. Yes, you can make the process shorter and easier. In most cases, however, short and easy searches result in a candidate who isn't right for the position. More and more, you hear about companies who completed an outside search in record time (a few weeks) or board members who are quoted as saying, "We knew even before we started the search that [blank] was the right choice." As nice as it would be to do a quick search that snared the right candidate, it rarely happens. Instead, a company selects an individual who appears to be qualified or has a great track record. To all outward appearances, he does seem to be a great choice for CEO. But when you scratch the surface and do a little investigation, you discover that there's a significant mismatch: The new CEO lacks a skill essential for the company's new strategy, or his leadership style isn't a good fit for a culture that the board feels must be maintained. As obvious as these mismatches might seem, they often don't show up at first or even second glance. It takes the right people asking the right questions and evaluating the answers perceptively to identify when a candidate doesn't fit. When companies take shortcuts, they miss a lot.

The Good Trend: Broadening the
Definition of Corporate Governance

Boards have been "outed" as a rubber stamp for the CEO in matters of management succession and CEO selection. The criticism they've received has spurred a number of boards to take on a more significant role in these processes. Media, shareholder, and investor scrutiny of the board's role has intensified, especially in light of the recent spate of CEO failures. Fortunately, man learns best from meaningful failure, and organizations are starting to recognize the need to expand the definition of corporate governance to include succession and selection responsibilities. Of course, boards would take on this role more readily if vested interest groups such as The Business Roundtable and the Hudson Institute fostered a culture that gave high marks to boards who developed and selected high-performing CEOs.

Nonetheless, it's a great sign that boards are becoming more aware of the need to expand their governance roles. Ideally, they'll continue to expand them in the following directions:

• *Embrace rather than shy away from the chance to be on a CEO search committee.* For many board members, this is a "hot potato" assignment they'd prefer not to touch. This reluctance to serve turns the assignment into a chore, and search committee members move forward reluctantly rather than with enthusiasm and energy. Once they're willing to take on their CEOs in terms of management succession and accept that this is part of good governance, they'll contribute more to the process.

• *Be more proactive about succession.* Selecting the next CEO isn't limited to voting for the best candidate. The responsibility should start long before this vote. Ideally, boards will become involved years before. This means that they'll invite prospective internal candidates to make presentations so they get to know them and watch them grow over time. This means that they'll make an effort to understand the company's strategy and culture in order to select a candidate that fits. Rather than waiting for candidates to be presented to them, they should make it their business to get involved as soon as possible.

- *Engage in straight talk with the CEO.* To expand their role, board members must be willing to confront the CEO when they feel his internal choice doesn't meet the specs or when he's intruding on the external CEO search process. As I've noted throughout the book, this can be extremely difficult for board members who feel personally and professionally connected to the CEO. Emotionally healthy CEOs, however, will recognize that straight talk is crucial, especially in the search for a successor.

- *Resist growing clones.* This is what AT&T's, Hewlett-Packard's, and IBM's boards countenanced, much to their chagrin. In a world that's rapidly changing, clones don't cut it. As successful as the previous CEO might have been, there's no guarantee that his success will be repeated if his successor is the same type of leader with the same type of background. Boards need to resist this cloning tendency by being acutely aware of strategic issues. When they know how a market is changing (or can make a good guess how it will change) and how a company must position itself for future growth, they can make cogent arguments for selecting a CEO who is different from the previous ones.

The Thin Line Between a Healthy Ego and a Dysfunctional One

In the future, I trust that boards will be less willing to accept a CEO who has crossed the line. In the past, they tended to look the other way when a CEO was abusing rather than using his power, and rationalized that this behavior comes with the territory. Great CEOs have always had healthy egos; they've always liked to control things; they've always been a bit temperamental. As a result, boards have traditionally bowed to "imperial" CEOs, especially when it came to the matter of choosing their successors.

They should bow no more. If they do, they are essentially bowing out of the selection and succession process. To select the right CEO today, objectivity is critical, and dysfunctional CEOs lack this objectivity. Boards need to assess whether they have an oblivious narcissist on their hands, a chief executive whose very success has warped his judgment. To make this assessment, consider the following list of personality traits:

- Must win at almost any cost
- Possesses an enormous need for power
- Insists on maintaining a clear-cut authority
- Enjoys unrealistic self-confidence
- Is totally independent
- Likes to be alone
- Can withdraw from family and friends easily
- Thrives on pressure
- Has flexible values

Most CEOs possess some if not most of these traits. Problems arise, however, when they possess one or more of these traits in excess. This is a sign that they've crossed over the line, and boards must be vigilant for these signs. When leaders move from being confident leaders to narcissists, it's highly unlikely that they will make wise decisions on their successor. When they surround themselves with weak people and start bullying instead of influencing others, they are dysfunctional CEOs who will sabotage the process. Some try to wrest control of selection away from the board. Others unilaterally choose an internal candidate they've been grooming for years, and never formally measure him against the specs or allow the board to participate in the decision. Still others retire in name only and undermine the new CEO's ability to perform effectively.

Boards are getting savvier and less inbred, and when they take their governance responsibilities seriously, they will prevent this dysfunctional CEO from harming the company for years to come.

Hopeful Signs

Though boards bear the brunt of responsibility for selecting a CEO, they can't do it alone. In fact, the boards that perform best are the ones where the other four players in the dynamic fulfill their roles. They provide a crucial balance, helping the board every step of the way and preventing them from going off track. While these four players still have a way to go before they become an ideal balancing force, they've made progress. Specifically

- *Incumbent CEOs are more aware that the leadership bar has been raised and changed.* It's the rare CEO who still hides in his sanctum sanctorum or is oblivious to the board's CEO selection responsibilities. As we move away from the traditional command-and-control leadership model, CEOs are starting to be less narcissistic and insistent that they name their successors. Though CEOs are naturally going to want to influence much of what takes place on their watch, they have also read the stories about the downfall of "all-powerful" CEOs. Astute chief executives recognize that the needs of their organizations have changed and will continue to change, and that if they were to clone themselves, they would not create the best CEO for the company's future. Ideally, this recognition will make them more diligent about crafting a good succession process and working with boards, CHROs, search consultants, and CEO candidates so that their successor is the right one.
- *CHROs are more likely to be included as part of the management team than in the past.* Although human resources professionals still are viewed in some companies as administrators (and sometimes deservedly so), the function has moved beyond the old policy wonk status and is seen as a key to attracting and developing talent. At a time when everyone is talking about the importance of human assets and a war for talent is raging, HR is no longer the black sheep of the

corporate family. Given the function's improved image, CHRO's have a better platform to confront the CEO when he's ignoring or deceiving the board about succession issues. Though I would not be so optimistic to state that many or even a majority of CHROs would be willing to confront their bosses over this matter, it's fair to say that more would be willing to do so today than in the past.

- *CEO candidates are becoming a bit less naive.* At the very least, they have become a bit more sophisticated about how the process works and the pitfalls along the way. Most candidates are smart enough to ask for date-certain retirements in writing and the role the incumbent will play once the transfer of power is completed. Certainly there will always be CEO candidates who will accept any conditions to obtain the CEO title. At the same time, people are becoming more realistic about the pros and cons of being CEO, and they realize that it's an increasingly tough job. Therefore, candidates will be more likely to make sure they know exactly what the job will involve (including the incumbent's future role) before they accept it.

- *The number of highly skilled executive search consultants is growing.* Although their number is counterbalanced by the book-and-bill mentality of too many search consultants, the fact remains that experienced CEO search consultants do exist. They understand how to help organizations make the right match between the specs and the individual. There are also consultants who have the integrity to walk away from a search when they know the game is "fixed" and that they will not be allowed to make the right match.

Do They Have What It Takes to Be CEO?

Boards must exercise even more diligence now than in the past in selecting a CEO. A lazy board or a compliant one won't be able to ask the tough questions or be sufficiently objective to find the candidate who is best suited to lead their company through challenging times. It's a mistake to underestimate these challenges or assume any reasonably competent executive can lead an organization.

Especially when a company is looking at outside candidates—where there are more question marks about candidate qualifications and credentials—they must be extraordinarily diligent or risk making a poor choice.

In the future, new criteria will be established for the CEO position. No doubt, certain competencies and experiences will be more important as markets, technologies, and economies change. I would not presume to create a list of future competencies, since my crystal ball isn't that clear. I would presume, however, to create a list of qualities that boards should screen for when conducting a CEO search. Though market conditions might change, the following six qualities will be very much in demand for years to come:

- *Strategic acumen.* Relatively few organizations will escape having to make significant strategic shifts in the coming years. Have candidates participated in or led a major shift before? Do they possess the vision to reinvent the company if necessary? Do they have the talent for analyzing the external economic and competitive vectors that influence corporate growth? Candidates may be financial geniuses or marketing mavens, but these skills are no substitute for strategic acumen.

- *Straight-talk capabilities.* Boards will unknowingly interview candidates who come from cultures where they were taught to hide information from board members as well as others within the organization. They will interview talented, intelligent people who simply are incapable of being up-front about bad news. Straight talk at the top of the organization filters down and encourages similar honesty and openness from the bottom up. Getting the facts straight is essential in an era where decisions must be made quickly.

- *Followership creators.* I would not want a coldly brilliant CEO leading my company who people respected but would never rally around. This doesn't exclude "tough" CEOs; it simply excludes ones who fail to inspire and motivate. Boards should investigate whether people love to work for a candidate; they need to discover whether former peers, employees, and customers provide glowing references. To retain talented people and to extract great productivity from them in highly competitive times, followership is required.

• *Verifiable experience.* Some CEO candidates exaggerate their skills and accomplishments; others are outright dishonest about them. This requires diligence. Boards should make it their business to verify if what they or their profiles say is true. The last thing boards want is to select someone who lacks international experience (though claims he has it) to head an organization intent on global expansion. Though a CEO may have been able to "fake it" in the past, that's no longer possible. Boards should question candidates about specific situations from their past that apply to the company's current requirements. If candidates evade these questions, that's a good indication they don't possess the requisite experience.

• *Courage.* By courage, I mean the ability to pull the trigger. I've seen too many CEOs freeze when it came time to make an important decision; they ended up agonizing over it and ultimately lost out because they couldn't decide with sufficient speed. The decisions facing CEOs today are tough ones: whether to make a commitment to e-commerce, whether to downsize the workforce, whether to merge or acquire, and so on. The CEO position is not for the faint of heart, and boards must use their experience and instincts to get a feel for how courageous candidates really are.

• *Culture fit.* Before assessing this quality, boards must determine whether they need a CEO who can fit into the culture or one who can shake it up and forge a new one. More so than ever before, companies—even highly successful, older ones—are realizing that their cultures have to change for them to be successful in the future. Commonly, a "gentlemanly" culture has to be made more risk-seeking and open, or a homogeneous culture has to become more diverse. It may be that a company needs a change agent rather than a CEO who seems as though he's been with the company all his life. In short, the board must seek the candidate who is best suited not for the present culture but for the future one.

I recognize that I'm asking a lot from boards as well as the four other players in the selection dynamic. Essentially, what I'm asking for is time, diligence, energy, and honesty. This is a big change for some people and organizations, especially those that have functioned as autocracies or gentlemanly cultures for years. It's difficult for a board member who feels indebted to the CEO to challenge his preferred candidate. It's a problem for an incumbent CEO to let go of the organization and allow his successor to do his job unimpeded. It's hard for CEO candidates who are close to their dream of being CEO to insist on certain conditions, no matter how reasonable. It's difficult for search consultants to shun a search they know they shouldn't take and for CHROs to help the board do its selection job and possibly displease the CEO in the process.

Despite these difficulties, I believe that most organizations are fully capable of selecting the right CEO. After all is said and done, it really comes down to a commitment to straight talk and taking the time to do things right. With that commitment in place, organizations will find the leaders who are best suited to meet their requirements.

Acknowledgments

I was mentored by some of the founders of the executive search profession. Harvey Stenson was my first boss at consultants A. T. Kearney, and I learned the art of client handling from Burnell Helmich of Helmich, Miller & Pasek. I first heard the phrase "We're Ivory Hunters, not Headhunters" from my friend Gardner Heidrick, the cofounder with John Struggles of what remains today one of the premier search consultancies. I salute their legacies.

I met Clarence McFeely in 1964 at A. T. Kearney, and we subsequently cofounded our executive search consultancy in 1969. For more than thirty-five years we worked together seamlessly, proving that a friendship founded on business is superior to a business founded on friendship. Thank you, Mac, for being my friend and partner. I also wish to thank my colleagues Mel Shulman, Roger Sekera, Bob Callan, and Charlie Jett, from whom I learned a great deal, as well as our researchers Marianne Dewey and Deborah Marshall.

Special appreciation goes to my valued assistant, Audrey Lehmann, who put up with my intransigence and was my backbone. I am thankful for the conversations with the late Don Baiocchi, who along with Ed Ruda stimulated my early interest in dysfunctional executive behavior, and to Linda Provus McElroy, Ph.D., and Ross McElroy, M.D., for their tutorial on the oblivious narcissistic personality. Thanks to Tom Wheeler for allowing me to share the "Blue Chip" story. And to my best friend and best critic, my wife Barbara Provus—an excellent search consultant in partnership with Dan Shepherd and Dave Bueschel—thank you, Barbara, for helping keep me humble.

Our lives are thus framed by our relationships. I am fortunate to have worked with wonderful clients and candidates, without whom I would not have enjoyed my gratifying career in search. I thank the following people for their interaction, friendship, and support: Maura Abeln, senior vice president, General Counsel, Owens Corning Corp.; the late Fred Aberlin, founder, Berry, Henderson & Aberlin; Dick Abington, formerly of General Electric Aerospace; Susan Alfano, senior vice president, human resources, MassMutual Financial Group; Jim Arnold, former head of the search practice, A. T. Kearney; Ken Bate, partner, JSD Partners; Hank Bowman, former CEO, Outboard Marine Corp.; Mike Bulkin, former director, McKinsey & Co.; Frank Burke, vice president, human resources, Biogen, Inc.; Bob Burt, chairman, FMC Corp.; John Butler, executive vice president, human resources, Textron, Inc.; Mike Callahan, former CFO, FMC Corp.; Lewis Campbell, chairman, Textron, Inc.; Bill Chambers, former chief human resources executive, GATX Corp.; David Chemerow, board member, Playboy Enterprises, Inc.; Paul Clark, chairman, ICOS Corp.; Art Collins, CEO, Medtronic, Inc.; Joe Cook, chairman, Amylin Pharmaceuticals, Inc.; Mike D'Ambrose, executive vice president, human resources, Toys R Us; Andre de Bruin, CEO, Quidel Corp.; Roxanne Decyk, chief strategy officer, Shell Corp.; Ed Dunn, former chief human resources officer, Whirlpool Corp.; Shel Erikson, chairman, Cooper Cameron Co.; George Farnsworth, former CEO, General Electric Aerospace; Janet Fiola, vice president, human resources, Medtronic, Inc.; Cary Fitchey, FG Ventures LLC; Bob Fowler, former chairman, IMC Global; Bill George, chairman, Medtronic, Inc.; Bob Goergen, chairman, Blyth Industries, Inc.; Don Grierson, CEO, ABB Vetco Gray, Inc.; Jim Hardymon, former chairman, Textron, Inc.; Christie Hefner, chairman, Playboy Enterprises, Inc.; John Herrell, chief administrative officer, Mayo Clinic, Mayo Foundation; Glen Hiner, chairman, Owens Corning Corp.; Bob Hoffman, former chairman,

Harnischfegger Corp.; Carroll Houser, former chief human resources executive, G.E. Medical Systems; Lowell Jacobsen, former chief human resources officer, Medtronic, Inc.; John Janitz, president, Textron, Inc.; Roger Kenny, managing director, Boardroom Consultants; Jay Kirby, former chief administrative officer, FMC Corp.; Carl Lehmann, chairman, RTW, Inc.; Sam Licavoli, chairman, Textron Automotive Corp.; the late Greg Liemandt, former chairman, UCCEL Corp.; Russ Lockridge, vice president, human resources, Brunswick Corp.; Warren Lyons, former chairman, Textron Financial Corp.; Art Marks, general partner, New Enterprises Association; Scott Marks, former vice chairman, First Chicago Corp.; Chip McClure, president, Federal Mogul Corp.; Jim McNerney, chairman, Minnesota Mining & Manufacturing Corp.; Dick Medland, former chief human resources officer, Outboard Marine Corp.; Gerry Miller, former chief administrative officer, Booth Newspapers, Inc.; Ron Mitsch, former vice chairman, Minnesota Mining & Manufacturing Corp.; Tim Moen, executive vice president, human resources, BANK ONE Corp.; Leo Mullin, chairman, Delta Air Lines, Inc.; Mike Murray, vice president, human resources, FMC Corp.; Gerry Nadig, chairman, Material Sciences Corp.; Glen Nelson, vice chairman, Medtronic, Inc.; Bob O'Connell, chairman, MassMutual Financial Group; Doug Pertz, chairman, IMC Global, Inc.; Larry Phillips, former chief human resources officer, Citigroup, Inc.; Hank Pietraszek, former CEO, Ventana Medical Systems; George Rathmann, former chairman, ICOS Corp.; John Reed, former chairman, Citicorp; Geoff Rehnert, cofounder, Audax Group; Roy Roberts, chairman, M-Xchange.com; Mitt Romney, founder, Bain Capital; Steve Rothschild, chairman, Twin Cities Live; Bob Ryan, senior vice president and CFO, Medtronic, Inc.; Jack Schuler, chairman, Stericycle, Inc.; Howard Shapiro, executive vice president, Playboy Enterprises, Inc.; Bob Singleton, CEO, Russell-Stanley Corp.; Gary Snodgrass, chief human resources officer, Exelon Corporation; Fred Steingraber, chairman emeritus, Kearney Management Consultants; Terry Stinson, CEO, Bell Helicopter Textron, Inc.;

Bob Stocking, former vice president, sales and marketing, G.E. Medical Systems; Tim Sullivan, vice president, human resources, Philip Morris International, Inc.; Steve Thompson, chairman, Immtech International, Inc.; Jim Vincent, chairman, Biogen, Inc.; Rich Vitkus, general counsel, Zenith Corp.; Win Wallen, former chairman, Medtronic, Inc.; Bill Wayland, former chief administrative officer, Textron, Inc.; Lorna Wayland, former chief human resources officer, Textron, Inc.; Jack Welch, chairman, General Electric Company; Tom Wheeler, former chairman, MassMutual Life Insurance Co.; David Whitwam, chairman, Whirlpool Corp.; Ron Zech, chairman, GATX Corp.

Finally, I would like to thank David Snyder of *Crain's Chicago Business*, and my book team, led by Bruce Wexler of Bookwriters Anonymous and Susan Williams and her colleagues at Jossey-Bass. Without their capable assistance, my professional life works would not now be in print.

F. W.

About the Author

After a thirty-five-year career in executive search consulting, specializing in CEO succession, Frederick W. Wackerle is now a consultant to CEOs and boards. In this capacity, he coaches CEOs on making transitions out of their organizations and advises boards on CEO succession and, if needed, the selection of search firms. During his executive search consulting career, Wackerle's firm, McFeely Wackerle Schulman, was considered a leader in its field.

Fred Wackerle has counseled CEOs and successfully recruited CEO successors, senior officers, and board members for top companies such as Biogen, Inc.; Citicorp, Inc.; FMC Corp.; GATX Corp.; General Instruments Corp.; ICOS Corp.; IMC Global; MassMutual; Medtronic, Inc.; Owens Corning; Playboy Enterprises, Inc.; Textron, Inc.; Ventana Medical Systems, Inc.; and Whirlpool Corp.

Each year since John Sibbald's book *The New Career Makers* (which ranks search consultants in the United States) began publication, Wackerle has been named one of the nation's top five general management search consultants by CEOs, human resources officers, and other high-ranking executives at the nation's fifteen hundred largest public and private companies, a ranking that was noted in *Business Week* magazine. In 1991, Wackerle was honored with the Gardner Heidrick Award from the Association of Executive Search Consultants (AESC) for outstanding contributions to the executive search consulting profession. He also received an AESC Special Recognition Award in 1989.

Wackerle received his bachelor's degree from Monmouth College, in Monmouth, Illinois, where he serves on the board of trustees and has endowed the Wackerle Leadership Center. He is also on the board of directors of the Rehabilitation Institute of Chicago. A frequent contributor to articles and the op-ed pages of leading national business publications, Wackerle also can be found "talking management" in a column in *Crain's Chicago Business*. His wife, Barbara Provus, is an executive search consultant, and he has two daughters and four grandchildren.

Index